apartment
GARDENING

Plants, Projects, and Recipes for
Growing Food in Your Urban Home

Amy Pennington

SASQUATCH BOOKS
SEATTLE

Printed in the United States of America
Published by Sasquatch Books

15 14 13 12   9 8 7 6 5 4 3 2

Cover design: Anna Goldstein
Cover development: Jessika Merrill
Cover photographs: Della Chen
Interior design and composition: Jessika Merrill
Interior and cover illustrations: Kate Bingaman-Burt

Library of Congress Cataloging in Publication Data
Pennington, Amy
  Apartment gardening : plants, projects, and recipes for growing food in your urban home / Amy Pennington.—1st ed.
  p. cm.
Includes index.
ISBN 978-1-57061-688-4 (pbk.)
  1. Urban gardening. 2. Container gardening. I. Title. II. Title: Plants, projects, and recipes for growing food in your urban home.

SB453.P358 2011
635.091732—dc22   2010045289

Sasquatch Books
1904 Third Avenue, Suite 710
Seattle, WA 98101
(206) 467-4300
www.sasquatchbooks.com
custserv@sasquatchbooks.com

SUSTAINABLE FORESTRY INITIATIVE
Label applies to the text stock
Certified Fiber Sourcing
www.sfiprogram.org

Contents

Acknowledgments

I would like to thank my daddio, Seth Dorian Pennington, Jr., for having an insatiable verve for living off the land, so much so that in retirement he moved himself, his lady, and a herd of goats out to the countryside of Pennsylvania and nestled them all against the banks of a mountain-fed stream.

Thank you to the team at Sasquatch Books who kept our garden conversation alive and well over many growing seasons—Gary Luke and Susan Roxborough. To Michelle Hope Anderson for her patience and help, and especially to Whitney Ricketts for yelling at me over a martini to "Write the damn book, already!"

Super big fat thank-you to the awesome design team that put their hot little hands on this book—designer Jessika Merrill and illustrator Kate Bingaman-Burt.

I owe a huge, huge thank-you to Patric Gabre-Kidan, one of my very best friends and an overall Mr. Fix-It who has been the most incredible teacher over the years. He has single-handedly taught me how to change a tire, hold a chef's knife properly, and build my own vegetable planter box. He is my superhero.

Thank you to John Chaffetz, who started out as a garden client, and grew into an extraordinary friend and collaborator. Brainstorms, laughter, and good food are never in short supply when he is around.

Big thanks and some serious neighborly love to my fellow apartment dwellers: Katie Okumura, who always offers to water my plants when I'm gone, and Frank Martin, who always lets me squeeze a few extra things into his fridge when mine is (more often than not) overflowing with food. And thanks to Jacci and Ann-Marie with whom I trade flowers and food with often. Viva La Tara!

Farm thanks to Luke Woodward and Sarah Cassidy, who run Oxbow Farm. They taught me, early on, how to sow seed and time my plantings. They are brilliant, and I love them.

I have so much gratitude for Lucio and Marta Dalla Gasparina, who had the excellent idea that I should grow their Nonna's Italian tomatoes in their yard for them. They didn't know they were creating a monster and lighting a spark in my life, and for that I am eternally grateful.

Double special thanks to Lynda Oosterhuis for always sharing her cooking secrets. She is one of the most amazing cooks I know.

As always, thank you to my family: Mom, Stacy, Seth, Gram, and the gaggle of nieces and nephews who crack me up daily. Love and thanks to my BK family: David, Carol, Dan, and Lil.

And finally, thank you to anyone reading these thank-yous! Your interest in and support of all things urban farm and garden are utterly inspiring. Keep growing!

Introduction

I am an urban gardener. Some may think of me as an urban farmer, depending on how you differentiate between a farm and a garden. I grow food for people in their city backyards, front yards, side yards, you name it: any patch of land in which I can persuade food to grow. And by food, I mean greens, roots, fruits, herbs, flowers, and more. My hope is to inspire people to eat a broader range of food and flavors than they are used to. I also want to evoke a sort of small-scale self-sufficiency in the daily lives of urbanites. People are sometimes inspired by what I do, but I'm not especially gifted in any way. I've killed damn near every houseplant I've ever owned, so I wouldn't say I was born with a green thumb. And I don't have a lengthy résumé in agriculture or horticulture. I am no expert at identifying plants, and I certainly don't ever remember the Latin names. Really, I just like food. A lot. So I want to have a steady supply of fresh and delicious produce as often as possible. I am motivated by my hunger, and so I grow food.

The ironic thing about my story is that, at present, I do not actually have a garden of my own. I live in a small apartment in Seattle with no access to a backyard, a lawn, or even green space. And though I often dream of tearing up my assigned parking spot and building a raised vegetable bed in its place, I don't think my landlord would appreciate the effort. So like most city people in search of greener pastures, I make do with what I have: in my case, an east-facing deck that gets the first rays of morning sun. Over time, I have overcrowded this tiny 75-square-foot space with pots, containers, hanging baskets, window boxes, and more. (I also use my dining room table as a greenhouse in the winter, which means inviting plants to further encroach on what little personal space I have.) I originally started with flowers and killed a good number of them. I now know that I wasn't watering efficiently, or the pots were too small, but at the time I just chalked it up to a big experiment.

My relationship with plants changed when I was asked to build and plant an organic vegetable garden for a food-loving Seattle couple. They hoped to grow the same tomatoes their Nonna grew in Italy. While I had little firsthand knowledge on how best to do this, I thought it sounded like an awesome challenge, so I dug in. Putting my hands in the dirt for the first time and sowing seeds was immediately very natural for me. I remember looking up at my friend Marcus (who worked with me that first year) and saying, "Marcus, this is the most instinctual thing I've ever done." I didn't have to think about it. I just planted. And like most new gardeners, I was shocked and amazed when those little green seedlings started pushing out of the soil. Nearly everything came up that year, and the garden was a huge success.

From then on, I was officially a grow-your-own convert, and I started experimenting with all sorts of plants. I grew spices, ate flowers, sowed Asian greens (some names of which I still can't pronounce), tried ten varieties of paste tomatoes, and more. The more time I spent in the garden, the more obvious the life cycle of plants became. I learned what it meant to overwater or underwater. I did plant trials in each of the raised beds to see how sun patterns would affect growth. All in all, I became really good at growing food efficiently and maximizing space. It was like a little game I played with myself—*how much food can I grow in this small space in the shortest amount of time?*

After that first year (and after getting used to bringing home some of the garden's bounty), I quickly tired of running across town to clip a handful of thyme for dinner. I refused to buy herbs at the grocery when I had fresh herbs to pick, but the back-and-forth car trips demanded too much energy—I disliked having to plan meals too far ahead, and being environmentally minded I felt guilty for burning the fuel. In the length of a summer, I slowly transitioned all of the flower pots at my apartment to containers of edible plants. Today, my deck overflows with pots, soil, and plants. I still have a thyme plant from that first garden thriving in a big terra-cotta pot on my balcony. I didn't really think about the transition happening just outside my door—it just happened organically.

In truth, I have grown food and plants far longer than my short adult history would suggest. I grew up in the wilds of Long Island in New York. My parents had defected from Brooklyn and Queens to live a simple life out in the "country." And although my childhood home sat within spitting distance of the Long Island Expressway, it really did feel like country. Our house was tucked in at the edge of a dead-end street. The yard was backed by a few acres of wooded land with meandering trails. The front yard started off like any old front yard, full of willow trees and a green lawn to run and do somersaults across, but over time my dad transitioned it to a working homestead. He built a gated pen for milk goats and another one for our pig, Maggie. We had rabbits for meat up in hutches, and one year we raised commercial turkeys for Thanksgiving, selling them to all his city friends. Muscovy ducks just sort of wandered around the yard, laying eggs where they saw fit. We would clip their wings every couple of months because if we didn't, they had a tendency to fly up and perch on the neighbor's roof. There was a large coop for the chickens, though they had free rein and could easily be corralled back to the coop at night.

In the backyard sat my parents' pride and joy: a huge vegetable garden. I remember my father renting a rototiller and turning over the turf one summer. As kids, we were utterly disinterested, but looking back now, I think my parents were superheroes. They tilled up the grass and hoed in rows like real live farmers. No raised beds, no fancy "garden," just row after row of vegetables. I have pictures of them hunched over rows of beans, while we kids are sitting in the shade in bathing suits doing nothing. Looking back now, I see that it was also one big adventurous experiment for my parents. Like most new gardeners, we had far too many zucchini. My dad would send us round the neighborhood to pawn them off on other families. I was so embarrassed once when I was refused. Tomatoes came in excess, sunflowers got eaten by birds (and their seeds did *not* taste like sunflower seeds from the store, so we snubbed them), and snap peas were my favorite.

My brother, sister, and I had weekly chores that, like most children, we dreaded. Unlike most of our friends with standard-issue duties, our burgeoning homestead kept us busy collecting eggs, milking the goats, tending to the other animals, and working in the vegetable garden out back. You can imagine the chore list come weekends. Someone had to clean out the goat shed, someone had to turn the compost pile we kept in the chicken coop, and someone had to weed. I remember sitting on a small bench in the garden and ripping out weeds, leaving some roots behind, and feeling both guilty and utterly empowered. I smugly left small pieces of dandelion root, knowing they would come back again to taunt us. (Sorry, Dad!) Above all other chores, I hated working in the garden.

While I hated garden work as a kid, I clearly found my calling as an adult. These days, I can be found in a garden any given day of the week, and I am continually drawing on my youth as a reference point. I wouldn't trade the way my parents raised me for the world.

Chapter 1

Before You Begin: The Basics

Over the years, I have experimented with growing food in pots and containers. Living in a small apartment with limited space has forced me to get creative. You know that expression "Necessity is the mother of invention"? Well, my friend Jason Werle says, "Frustration is the mother of invention," and I couldn't agree more! I'll be the first to admit, pots are not my favorite way to grow food. But they work well enough, and I certainly can't complain about fresh salad greens just outside my door.

Contrary to recent popular belief, though, not all vegetables grow well in containers. Most plants can be grown in a pot; however, not all plants will come to full maturity and produce food in a pot. By planting in a pot you are inhibiting the plant's growth to some extent. Plants can send out roots and root hairs only as far as the walls of the pot allow. This presents the biggest challenge of growing food in small spaces. Growing food in pots and containers calls for a different mind-set than you need for growing food in the ground. However, armed with a little bit of information you can make educated decisions and increase your chances of success.

We tend to think about the dirt under our feet as just that—dirt. But soil is another matter. Without healthy soil, we would not be able to grow food. Natural soil is a living thing, with inherent qualities that are not readily available in a bag of potting soil. Potassium, nitrogen, microbial matter, phosphates, calcium, and other nutrients are present in natural soil in varying degrees. Soil breathes, grows, lives—and can die. Hundreds of articles have been written about the importance of healthy soil on a global level, and you should read them. Soil is crucial to our livelihood.

When you're growing food (or any plant) in a container, however, you don't use "soil." Instead, you use a potting mix—also called a soil *medium.* The density of this mix is lighter than garden soil and conditioned for containers. Therefore, container gardens run the risk of lacking all of those healthy minerals and living organisms that naturally occur in soil. To be a successful container gardener, you have to really think like a plant.

For a new gardener, it is helpful to recognize that information often varies from source to source. Also, it's good to note that gardening "experts" often use a combination of education and experience to offer advice and instruction on how to grow a bountiful garden. That doesn't necessary mean it will all work for you. I have opinions about what works and what doesn't, but there are many options for home gardeners. Gardening means working with nature, and this is not an exact science. There are far too many variables to be able to definitively state what will grow best where. Sun exposure, latitude, time of year, watering schedule—all of these things and more will affect the success of any planting you do. It depends on what you have to work with and your own preferences. For instance, I don't grow tomato plants in my apartment garden. Tomatoes need big pots, and my deck is already too small. Also, tomatoes are sun lovers, and I don't get enough sun. Even in the *best* conditions I would harvest only a few pints of cherry tomatoes from one plant. With all the nurturing and time that tomatoes need, it's just not worth it to me to bother. Especially when farmers' markets abound and I can pick up locally grown tomatoes each summer. So although certain factual information having to do with nutrient requirements won't change among the many books you can read, strategies will. It's up to you to decide what works best for you and your garden—and like me, you will learn your best lessons from experiments and experience.

Here I have distilled my cumulative experience in a variety of conditions over time in the hopes that this information will help you make good choices. You should read up on all the science-y stuff too. This books offers a basic overview of the important elements to gardening. To problem solve, you need to understand a plant's needs and why it behaves in certain ways. Although plants do a really good job of keeping themselves alive, it's smart to understand what is happening and how you can help them along. This foundation of basic knowledge is a great place to start.

In general, I take a fairly lazy approach to my apartment garden. The ultimate goal is for the garden to be productive. I want a constant supply of the ingredients I use often, and I want to nurture plants that can be continually harvested from. I want both plants that will run through their life cycle in one season as well as plants that are perennials and will continue to come back year after year. I try to mix reseeding plants and perennials with those annuals that must be planted anew each year, so I'm not starting completely from scratch every spring. It's a satisfying experience to see your garden getting started before you've even had time to think about planting and planning. *That* is the best kind of apartment garden: one that isn't too high-maintenance and can fend for itself when need be, all the while offering up fresh ingredients for your kitchen. Brilliant.

A successful apartment garden requires some thought and strategy. I often say choosing what to grow on my deck is like the *Sophie's Choice* of gardening—an impossible decision that must be made. I suggest growing plants that will be used frequently, but in small amounts. This gives plants time to regrow between cuttings. No sense in planting a crop that you'll wipe out in one go. I figure it's better to have something available over a long course of time. To that end, I rely heavily on herbs for the apartment garden. Herbs will single-handedly change the flavor of most recipes. Eaten fresh, or cooked over time, they impart a flavor that few other foods can. They are the quintessential kitchen ingredients, and the choices extend far beyond the commonly used thyme, rosemary, and sage.

I also grow plants that produce abundant quantities of ingredients that I know I'll use often. Lettuces, for example: these are wonderful to grow at home. They take up little space, produce (and reproduce!) quickly, and offer fresh greens for salads, or as a nice leafy garnish. I use lettuce in large amounts, and their leaves grow back quickly, making them highly productive, economical, and worthwhile. Therefore few other vegetable plants work especially well in containers, but there are a handful that are ideal for the small working space of apartment gardens.

Make the most of what you grow by considering its uses beyond the kitchen. Lavender makes for a subtle herb rub for seared duck breast and can also be used as a scented stuffing for an eye pillow. Scented geranium leaves can be chopped and used with sweet

---

GARDEN GLOSSARY 101

There are a number of gardening terms to familiarize yourself with, as well as some professional vocabulary that you should know before you get started.

Amendment: A beneficial ingredient added to the soil: fertilizer, compost, sand, and so on.

Annual: A plant that completes its life cycle in one season or year. Annuals must be reseeded (naturally or intentionally) in order to grow in subsequent years.

Cloche: A protective covering made of material, glass, or plastic meant to promote and foster healthy plant growth.

Cotyledon: The first, tiny leaves that develop on a seedling after germination.

Deadhead: To remove dead flower heads from a plant.

Guerilla gardening: The act of taking over abandoned or vacant land and growing plants without permission.

Hardening off: Slowly acclimating new plants to outdoor weather conditions by putting them outside for increasing lengths of time.

recipes, and they can also be infused into water for a facial toner. Or used for teas. Some plants are grown for leaves, some for seeds, and some for fruits. I try to round out my garden plan so there is always something to harvest from. Today, as I write this, I have lovage seeds, anise hyssop, nigella (love-in-a-mist), and scented geraniums. In three weeks the nigella will be gone, the lovage will be cut back, and I'll be harvesting a second crop of lettuce. A container garden should ebb and flow, just as a large garden would.

Having an apartment garden likely means your space is small. Outside of begging your neighbors for some prime deck real estate, take advantage of the wider urban garden available to you every day. Outside the confines of your compact garden lies a city full of wild edibles that often go neglected and undiscovered. When strolling about your city, keep your eyes peeled. You likely won't have to travel far to find something edible growing close by. Look on the

---

Overwinter: The duration of time from fall to spring for plants that can survive outside unprotected. Overwintering also refers to the process of putting plants under protective cover so they may survive the winter.

Perennial: A plant that lives longer than one growing season, typically for more than two years.

Phototropism: When a plant bends toward a light source.

Reseeding annual: An annual plant that drops seed on its own, thereby self-sowing for next year.

Rogue gardening: The act of dropping seed bombs or tossing seeds into open places hoping they will germinate and grow on their own.

Root-bound: When a plant outgrows its pot and the roots from the plant smash up against the container walls and twist around each other.

Runner: A plant that will send out roots from its stem to produce another plant that can be severed from the parent plant. Strawberries spread by runners.

Top-dress: To dress the top layer of soil surrounding a plant with fertilizer, mulch, or compost.

ground: windfalls from abandoned fruit and nut trees and wild greens are ready and accessible nearly all year long. Although foraging is a craft that is honed over time, anyone can spot and pick out a dandelion from a grassy field. Start your foraging adventures small. Pick what you know. Pretty soon, you'll be doing homework and gathering more plants to eat. (More on this in Chapter 8, Garden Lite.) Knowledge is an evolution, and nature provides the perfect seasonal timeline to learn from.

And really, that is what it's all about. Learning while you go. And grow! This book is meant as a beginner's guide, with everything you need to get started. All the plants you'll learn about here are easy, low bars of entry to gardening, and some projects don't even require potting soil—and will have you eating in days. They are not the most familiar edibles you may find, but they're all tasty and beautiful and seasonal and charming. I hope you'll dig in to one of these small projects now, and next year or next season you'll dig a little deeper. Trial and error are your best guides, particularly as no two gardens are created equal. Make the most of your space and see what happens.

And, most importantly, don't fret. Plants *want* to survive and live. They will go to great lengths to make sure their genetic strain lives on. They are genetically predisposed to grow big and strong so they can set seed and make more plants. They don't need constant monitoring—they just need a helper.

Have fun, do your best, and I bet you'll come out smelling like roses. And you know what? If you're just dying to grow a tomato on your patio, you should definitely go for it.

Chapter 2

Getting Grounded: Pots, Containers, Soil & Supplies

For beginning gardeners, or even those with a year or two under their belts, the world of garden tools, materials, and supplies can be overwhelming. I have stood in the garden aisles of home stores and nurseries, utterly baffled by the multitude of products available. I cannot imagine what it must feel like to try to sort through all that information and decide what essentials you need to get started and get growing.

The good news is you really don't need much, particularly for a small urban garden. Before you invest too much in supplies, determine whether your deck gets at least a few hours of sun. Ambient light may be OK to grow some herbs and potentially a lettuce or two, but you can kiss any thoughts of cucumbers and tomatoes good-bye. Sorry! And if you really don't get a lick of sun, check out your community gardening programs. Most cities offer up plots in community gardens, and often a neighbor is more than happy to share part of a yard. If, however, you have a minimum of six hours of sunlight, the world of edibles opens up to you. Tomatoes would still be a challenge, but herbs, leafy greens, and some fruiting plants like snap peas will grow.

To start a garden in containers, at a bare minimum you'll need pots, soil, and fertilizer. A bag of compost is a great addition, so you should purchase one of those when you're gathering supplies. (And see Chapter 5, Feeding & Watering Plants.) Access to water is also an important consideration. In my own garden, I fill eight old water bottles and carry them back and forth from my kitchen sink. In an apartment, it's usually not too far of a carry! Just make sure you have some way to water your plants, as containers require a diligent watering schedule. Small container gardens benefit from a few other supplies as well. These extras support your plants, help to prolong the growing season, and in general, make your life a little easier.

You might think choosing pots would be the easiest part of an apartment garden, but interestingly, it is not. Containers and pots come in many sizes and seemingly just as many materials. You can  look at your planting vessel in one of two ways—you can choose the pot first and then pick the best-suited plant, or buy the plant and then choose the best-suited pot. I find myself con-sistently drawn to the cutest little pots with the brightest colors, but they end up being fairly useless. Most plants need a little legroom to stretch their roots. Try to plant in a pot that's a bit bigger than the plant will actually need. It is better to leave a little wiggle room than to have plant roots mash-ing up against the container walls. If you allow for some growth, you increase the odds of your plant growing to full maturity. The end goal is for the plant to produce as much as possible. In Chapter 3, What to Grow, For Real, there are notes under each plant suggesting the most ideal container. Decide for yourself and know that everything is an experiment. You can always adjust next year, or transplant later in the season if you've underestimated.

If you have the energy and creativity to make your own contain-ers, go for it. Building a custom-made container gives you much more flexibility, as you ultimately control the width and depth. I prefer angular containers like squares and rectangles. This linear shape allows for row planting, even if on a small scale. Chapter 7, Do-It-Yourself Garden, has some basic instructions for a simple planter box. Traditional round pots tend to taper at the bottom, which helps with drainage but also crams the roots together. All in all, shoot for an equal mix of both container shapes.

Container material is an area where you need to make some personal choices. I love the look and feel of clay terra-cotta pots. They are uniform and shapely. They also come in a multitude of different sizes, so it's easy to overcrowd small spaces and have a variety of plants growing while still be pleasing to the eye. The consistency and repetition of the same pot gives a tidy appearance. Ceramic pots are a great option as well. They are typically glazed and add a bit of color to the garden. The downside of ceramic pots is that they can cost twice as much as their terra-cotta counterparts. But when you are

HAND-DRILLED DRAINAGE

If you start looking around town for various containers you can use on your patio for planters, you will likely find some pretty cool things. Amongst the jackpot items are ceramic pots. Glazed ceramic pots are more expensive then terra-cotta, so I rarely spend the money on them, but they add a splash of color and are so pretty they're hard to resist. But from time to time people *do* give these away. Just keep your eyes peeled. In the event that there are no drainage holes in these pots (which is often the case), you can actually drill your own. You need an electric drill and a special bit, but if you don't have your own set of electric tools, borrow them from someone and you're golden. The bigger the pot, the more holes you should have. Three to five per each pot is usually fine.

Here's how to drill drainage holes. Flip the pot over onto the lawn or a few layers of newspaper. (You want a soft surface to cushion the pot so you don't chip the edges.) Cover the area where you will drill the holes with a crisscross of masking tape. This helps to prevent splinters from flying up. Mark the holes on the tape. Using a drill fitted with either a ceramic or masonry bit, drill your hole. Try to work in one swift motion and drill straight down to minimize the chance of cracking the ceramic.

working in a small garden, aesthetics are important, so go ahead and add a touch of vibrancy here and there—just don't spend your entire budget on pots alone. One important note about ceramic pots: if you buy one without a drainage hole, have the nursery drill several, or make your own using an electric drill. Plants generally need good drainage to grow well; without it, a pot can easily get waterlogged, air doesn't circulate as readily, and it's hard to tell when the plant needs more water.

Recently I have started to add plastic pots to my container mix. Plastic is much lighter, so it's easier to lift when full of soil and shift its position for best sunlight than a clay pot, which is quite a bit heavier. (For a great project on how to get your plastic pots to not look so *plastic*, see Spray-Painted Containers on page 139.)

Pots and Containers

Sizes

Staring up at the walls of pots available for gardening can be a bit daunting. Don't freak out! Any old pot is better than no pot, though it is helpful to make a plan before you go shopping. Pots come in a variety of shapes and sizes and can be grouped simply into large, medium, and small. Keep those general terms in mind and make sure to pick up a variety of pots. Purchase one or two pots at a time to add to your garden each season. This gives you time to adjust to general garden care without being overwhelmed and spaces out your budget over several seasons.

Large pots

Large pots are those deeper than sixteen inches. Typically, both round pots and square containers come in widths proportionate to their depths. When purchasing large pots, opt for the largest one they have. For a visual cue, make a circle in front of your body with your arms, fingertips touching. This width is about the diameter of a large pot. Go big and try something a bit larger than what you had in mind. Most stores stock a wide variety of sizes, but in my experience, a larger pot will expand your gardening possibilities. They leave enough space for growth and will therefore support healthy and abundant plants. If you ever come across a large pot that someone is giving away, nab it!

Medium pots

Medium-sized pots run between eight and sixteen inches deep. Long, shallow pots are also considered "medium" due to the reasonable amount of space they allow for growing. Most people choose medium pots when they're shopping, but this size should be used only for smaller plants such as lettuce, mâche, or creeping herbs like thyme.

Small pots

These little one-plant pots are less than eight inches deep. I fill small, dainty pots with hardy herbs or single lettuce plants,

SMALL PLANTS FOR SMALL POTS

I'd like to reiterate that the size of the container will eventually affect the size a plant will grow. I'm not a huge fan of small pots for growing anything edible. The plants may not die, but certainly many will not come to full maturity if you inhibit their space in this way. Small pots will also dry out very quickly. In my own garden, the smallest pot I have used was about four inches deep and about that wide—I treated it as an experiment. Nothing really grew well in such a small space, and what little of the plant was alive was horribly root-bound, poor thing. Even lettuces, which are pretty tolerant, suffered in such tight confines. Their leaves never got bigger than baby lettuce size, and I wound up scrapping the whole project.

Very few plants work well in these conditions, but there are a few you can get away with. The smallest pot I would recommend would be six inches deep and about the same width. This size pot can accommodate one small plant. Just one! I can't tell you how many plants I've seen crammed into these tiny pots, and I promise you—they will not grow. (Unless you plan on going the microgreen route, in which you harvest plant starts when they are only an inch or two tall. In that case, you can fill the pot with seeds and, generally, harvest within two weeks.)

Shallow-rooted plants work best in small pots. Small pots can also accommodate plants that you do not need to harvest from often. Lemon balm, for instance, is quite hardy and will survive the tight conditions, though its leaves will be much smaller than those of a plant given room to reach its full potential. This doesn't matter so much for lemon balm, as it is a strong herb that will likely not be used frequently. Keep in mind, also, that small pots need lots of watering on hot days—likely at least twice a day.

The following is a list of some good plant options for smaller pots—as either they are shallow-rooted, or a kind of plant you will not use in large quantities and can harvest in smaller batches.

> **Lemon balm**
>
> **Microgreens: arugula, radish**
>
> **Scented mints: chocolate, pineapple, apple**
>
> **Strawberry**

accepting that they won't fully mature. Small pots are great for adding color and dimension to the garden and can be used to grow microgreens. In my experience, it's easy to be tempted into buying more small pots than you really need; remember, you can always go back for more.

Materials

Plastic

Plastic pots are the least expensive container option, so they're great for anyone on a budget. It's true that they are usually the least attractive option, and they do not weather in that lovely rustic way that ceramic pots do. On the plus side, however, plastic pots will hold their moisture longer than clay or ceramic pots. Again, plastic planters are lighter and easier to move around. I grow my lettuces in a long, narrow, shallow plastic pot that I gussy up with a coat of bright paint (see Spray-Painted Containers project on page 139).

Clay

Clay pots are porous, so air moves easily through their walls. This is helpful in that it allows roots to breathe and keeps them out of direct water, but it's not helpful in that the soil tends to dry out quickly. In hot weather you'll need to closely monitor the moisture in your clay pots. These pots are a fairly inexpensive option for the home gardener, after plastic ones, and they come in myriad shapes and sizes. If you choose clay pots, be sure to purchase a saucer or plate to sit under the pot. This works in two ways—to keep moisture off the surface of your deck or patio and to hold a bit of moisture for the plant.

Wood

Wooden boxes, whether purchased or built, are nice additions to the patio garden. They are perfectly angular and therefore easy to grow in and fit neatly into corners. They come in large sizes that give plants plenty of space. Wood withstands weathering over time, and even if the edges become slightly warped or dull, the plants in them will grow. I have had the same wooden boxes for well over seven years now, and they're still in decent shape. As with clay, the growing medium in wooden boxes will dry out a bit faster than in plastic, but the wood does tend to hold moisture a smidge longer.

Salvaged Materials

Every year, I e-mail a local restaurant and ask them to hold aside some asparagus crates for me. Asparagus is one of the first vegetables available in the Pacific Northwest in spring. That means the crates are available right about the time I start planting my springtime containers. The crates tend to be of pretty simple construction—compressed wood planks held together by loosely twisted wire. You need only fill the space between the planks to make a planter box for cheap! Fill the gaps with Spanish moss or coconut fiber lining, and voilà!—you have a deep container for your plants. There are lots of everyday items that can act as planters. Here are just a few to inspire you.

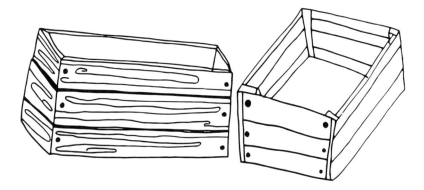

---- **Coffee or olive oil cans:**
Some people still buy their coffee in aluminum tins; these make awesome containers for lettuces. Be sure to punch holes in the bottom of the can with a thick nail to allow for drainage. And plant just one lettuce per can! Olive oil cans follow the same

guidelines. While these are not readily available to home cooks, ask at your local restaurant; they often buy olive oil in bulk, which comes in vibrant-colored tins.

---- **Five-gallon plastic pots:** These are the sturdy plastic pots that shrubs and other large nursery plants often come in. Granted, they're not the most attractive pots you can find to grow food in, but they are free, and most retailers simply dispose of them. Check with your local plant nursery to see whether they have extras, and put a call out to gardening friends come spring. Chances are someone will have extra for you. Spray paint the exteriors a color that pops, and soon enough you'll have a patio full of eye-catching pots.

---- **Gutters:** Found on nearly every building and home, gutters are easy to come by. This long and shallow material is perfect for planting lettuces. Be sure to drill drainage holes along the length of the gutter before filling with potting soil and planting. Because gutter material is light (stainless steel, aluminum, or plastic), this is an ideal planter for hanging off a railing, and it uses the small space of a patio efficiently. You can pick up any length at a salvaged materials depot or a local construction site. Look for one made of stainless steel—they are the best looking.

---- **Plastic milk crates:** Much like the asparagus crates, plastic milk crates make easy planters. You will need to fill in the gaps with either a liner (like a gently used plastic shower liner with drain holes), Spanish moss, or some sort of fiber—coconut fiber or even hay. I like to spray paint my milk crates white—this gives them a very clean, modern look.

---- **Wine boxes:** If you live in or near wine country, wooden wine boxes shouldn't be too difficult to find. These shallow boxes are good for lettuces, seed starting, and microgreens. The best way to get your hands on them is by calling around to wineries and asking if they have extra. The thin wood on these boxes will last longer if you apply a coat of oil before planting; this helps give your boxes a tough and slightly waterproof finish. Choose a Danish oil or orange oil from your local hardware store.

---- **Burlap, potting soil bags, and other sacks:** It has become the vogue to grow plants directly in a bag of potting soil. This process will work, but it does not make the most attractive container. If you are dying to give it a try, go for it. You need only steady the bag and split a hole in top, then add your starts or seeds.

For a plant-in-a-bag project, I prefer a better-looking bag. Burlap sacks and plastic woven feed bags are a bit more shabby-chic. If you live in an area with local coffee-roasting companies, you should be able to find used burlap bags for free. Check in with your local roaster early in the season or during winter for a guaranteed source. Country feed stores are a good source for old feed bags. These often have the added benefit of vintage-looking logos—a great way to add character to your urban garden.

To plant in these, simply pour an entire bag of potting soil into the burlap sack or feed bag. Plant starts or seeds directly on the soil surface and be sure the edges of the bag don't come up around the plant to block out sunlight. Soil kept in burlap will dry out quickly, so be sure to monitor water needs closely. The plastic feed bags will hang onto water as a plastic pot would, so be certain not to overwater these.

Soil

The matter of soil may seem pretty obvious. You can grab any ol' bag of potting soil and grow something in it. But all potting soils are not created equal. Potting soil mix should drain well while still holding moisture. Most soil mixes are formulated to maintain a certain level of lightness so that plants are able to breathe. Air is right up there with sun and water in importance to healthy, thriving plants.

Your potting soil should include a mix of compost or bark. These add richness and texture to the soil and will help to retain moisture. I recommend steering clear of any soil mixes containing peat or peat moss. Peat is not a sustainable resource, as it takes thousands of years to make. Although peat does a good job of establishing a good growing environment, there are other, more sustainable and natural products to look for. Coconut fiber is a great example. The porous fibers of the coconut hair absorb and hang on to water and also let air circulate through the soil.

Don't pay too much attention to all the marketing claims on some potting soil. "Slow release of water to roots," and all sorts of other grand claims are merely attempts to get you to buy a product. Look for organic potting soil mixes from smaller regional companies rather than the national brands you'll find in big-box stores.

Choose a potting soil that has no added fertilizer or nutrients. It is best to add those on your own as needed for the particular plants you will grow.

It is a good idea to mix a few handfuls of organic compost into the soil in each pot. You can do this when you first plant, or add a *top-dressing* of compost around the base of your plants as the potting soil settles. Plan to top-dress each container a couple of times a season. It will help soil hold on to moisture, which in turn will attract microorganisms. You'll find more information on keeping your soil in tip-top condition in Chapter 5, Feeding & Watering Plants.

Once you have a nice soil mix in your pots and are fertilizing at regular intervals, you can relax and let the plants do their thing. Each spring, however, it's a good idea to refresh the soil mix for any pots that have dead plants. Perennial plants that have been in the same pot for years will also benefit from fresh soil. I will often add fresh potting soil to older plants if the existing soil has become really dry and caked over time.

To do this, tip out the entire plant and free up any root balls that have formed. I work directly on my deck and keep a dishpan and brush close by for sweeping up any soil that gets away. Break up and loosen the root ball with your fingers to free up the soil and roots.

Then, scoop in enough fresh potting mix to cover the bottom of the container so that the plant stem is level with the container rim. Set down the plant and fill in the pot with fresh potting mix, holding the plant straight and firming the mix around the roots to stabilize it. Then water well. If the plant is severely root-bound, you may also loosen the roots as noted and transplant to a larger container.

Transplanting to a larger container will allow the plant to grow and thereby increase your overall harvest. You have to decide if transplanting is the best option for you. Want more production? Then the plant will need more space. If it produced the perfect amount of harvestable plant, you may use the same container.

When adding new plants to previously used containers, do not rely on simply digging a small hole in the soil and stuffing in a plant start. Old soils often contain dead roots from previous plants. Those roots will impede the new plant's roots and constrict air as the new plant tries to grow into the same small space. For that reason, just as in a field or on a farm, it's best to rework your soil before planting. Till your soil using a fork or your hands. Loosen it up, remove the root hairs, then gently work in some compost and a handful of fertilizer before adding a new plant start.

Supplies

The basics just described are all you absolutely need to grow food at home. Because you are working in a controlled environment by planting in containers, you can get away with far fewer tools and supplies than if you were growing food in a garden plot. However, there are many gardening tools and devices that can expand the possibilities of any gardening adventure.

Garden Gloves

A pair of lightweight gloves will protect your hands and nails from soil and rough plant materials and spare them from the drying effects of frequent washing and scrubbing. Potting soil, although not as "muddy" as topsoil, will get under your nails and into your pores, and it's hard to scrub out. There are many glove choices, but an inexpensive pair of lightweight canvas gloves will suffice for a small urban garden.

Floating Row Cover

Floating row cover is a thin sheet of spun polyester that can be used in several ways. You can lay the cloth directly over seeds and plants for protection and insulation. In the early spring and late fall, row cover helps warm up the soil. It is also a good protector against garden pests. Pests like slugs and aphids are not typically a problem for apartment gardeners, but they have shown up on my deck on occasion—and I live three floors off the ground! Birds and wildlife may sometimes visit your pots and toss the dirt around while looking for food. Floating row cover deters them from rooting around in your plants. In the heat of the summer, if you have full sun exposure, you may need to provide your plants with shade. Stretching this cloth either over your pots like a tent or as a screen across your entire patio will help keep plants cool. Think of it as a protective umbrella for your plants.

Trellis

A structured trellis will offer support to any climbing or tall plants and is perfect for maximizing and managing your space. Cucumbers, peas, and nasturtiums are great for training up a trellis. Also, plants growing up a trellis offer subtle and lush privacy between neighbors in apartments or condos. Even if plants die back, a trellis is an excellent addition to the garden design as a vertical element, so be sure to choose a sturdy and attractive trellis structure that you won't mind looking at once winter arrives and the trellis is left bare.

Bamboo

Bamboo is like the duct tape of gardening—it has many uses. Use single stakes to support heavy plants, assemble a trellis, or form a teepee by tying twine or wire at the top. You can also easily build a shade wall for blocking out the strong summer sun—wrap floating row cover between two bamboo stakes and secure. Keep a few bamboo stakes of different lengths around. Most hardware stores sell six-foot lengths of sturdy bamboo that you can cut to any desired length with a handsaw. Bamboo is also available in shorter, thinner stakes that are more flexible and will not require cutting.

Potting Table

I have always wanted a potting table. You can work directly on the floor of your deck or patio; this is a fine and functional option. But a potting table frees up some space and will help keep things organized. These hip-height wonders are the perfect place to turn out soil, store extra pots, and shelve or hang any equipment and supplies you have. If you have the space and budget for a potting table, I highly recommend getting one.

Chapter 3

What to Grow, For Real

Growing plants in containers is a tricky thing. There are plenty of resources available about growing food in containers that imply that this process is simple and straightforward—but most of us will find that it takes some trial and error.

My own experience is probably somewhat typical of what you can expect. Over the years, I've tried a mix of plants in a mix of containers and finally settled into a routine of what I grow. I steer clear of plants that won't produce much in a container or that have too long of a growing season. I find it best to focus on plants that are either very versatile in their culinary uses or will produce a generous harvest in a short amount of time. I use my apartment garden as creative inspiration for my meals, so I like to keep a little bit of a lot of different things.

Again, growing plants in a small space inhibits their growth potential. To understand why, it is helpful to understand the root systems of plants. This knowledge is of practical importance for gardeners—even novice gardeners who are just dabbling with growing food at home. As you begin to grasp basic growing concepts, it is much easier to make educated guesses on how best to grow successfully in your apartment garden. You don't need to get super science-y

LET'S GROW!

BUY or MIX POTTING SOIL

+

GET A POT

+

OAK LEAF

SEEDS

+

WATER

=

GROW!

about it, but it is quite helpful to know just what is happening underneath the surface of your soil.

When a seed is first planted, a root is formed and begins to grow downward, sending out what is known as the *taproot*. This taproot will typically extend deep into the soil; it forms the beginnings of a plant's main root stem, from which smaller roots form and branch outward. These *root hairs* are like our own capillaries, fanning out horizontally and sometimes downward from the main root. Root hairs grow at various depths along the root system. Some branch out and spread wide just under the surface; others may form and branch out deeper in the subsoil.

This basic root system—encompassing the main root stem and its branch-like root hairs—has some very basic and obvious functions: absorbing nutrients and water for the plant. This happens most often in deep soil. The taproot is responsible for taking up nutrients. If you've ever transplanted a tree or shrub, you may have seen instructions to add fertilizer to the freshly dug hole. This is why. The deeper the fertilizer, the more readily available it is as food for the plant. Roots then store both nutrients and water to feed the plant. (Chapter 5, Feeding & Watering Plants, has all the information needed to make sure plants are getting the proper nutrition for healthy growth.)

Without a strong root system, it is nearly impossible for any plant to grow to maturity. Sometimes, although we may interrupt the natural process of a plant life cycle, we are still able to harvest. For example, romaine lettuce grown in a shallow container may not grow to a full-sized leaf, but it will still grow and be plentiful. It is a delicate balance between giving the plant enough space to produce and making certain there is enough to harvest.

The following suggestions on what to grow in your apartment garden are based on plants that will do best in the sorts of pots and containers available to you at nurseries and retail shops, or by using little odds and ends you can turn into containers. There are plenty of plants that will do well in large container boxes six feet long and three feet deep. For an urban garden, however, I am assuming that the space you have to grow in is quite small. Additionally, these suggestions are based on plants that I have found to be great producers. You will be able to grow and harvest from these plants multiple times. They have earned their keep on my Must-Grow list. I have intentionally excluded plants that will produce in mediocre proportions, as well as plants that aren't guaranteed to be delicious. It is also good to note that I'm defining a "good producer" as a plant that will serve you several times. For that reason, I steer clear of most sautéing greens—they cook down too much to warrant the time and energy it takes to nurture in a pot. Of course, if you want to plant an urban farm in a multitude of containers, have at it!

With that, the following are some of my apartment favorites.

Fruits and Vegetables

Vegetables are essentially the "meat and potatoes" of an apartment garden. These plants will add sustenance to your table and help make a meal. When the cupboards are bare, you should be able to rely on the garden to come through and provide some key fresh ingredients that will inspire a meal.

Vegetable plants have higher nutrient needs than herbs and flowers, so you will have to be mindful of fertilizing. I recommend keeping some sort of log so you know when to fertilize again. (I do this by creating an appointment in my online calendar every six weeks or so.) Different plants, too, have varying requirements—but will need some combination of nitrogen, phosphorus, and potassium: NPK. Leafy greens need plenty of nitrogen (N), as nitrogen supports leafy green growth in all plants. Fruiting plants grown for their fruits (like peas or cucumbers) rather than for their leaves or roots require more phosphorus (P).

Potassium (K) is needed in small amounts by all kinds of plants for strong and consistent root growth and overall plant health. As plants have individual requirements, I buy my fertilizer components in bulk and tailor the proportions specifically to each pot. You can read more about how to properly feed your plants in Chapter 5, Feeding & Watering Plants.

You need to be especially mindful of watering your vegetable plants. If you stress the plant by under- or overwatering, odds are it won't produce as expected. Although herbs will bounce back from neglect over time, with vegetables you run the risk of damaging the plant beyond repair. More information on watering can be found in Chapter 5, Feeding & Watering Plants.

Harvesting from your plants is one of the single most important things you can do. A plant's life cycle is such that it grows to maturity and sets seed so that future generations can live on. By interrupting this process (halting its ability to make seeds by harvesting) you ensure that the plant will continue the cycle a little bit longer. In a funny way, you are making the plant stress that it will not survive. Plants are genetically disposed to keep striving to produce offspring so that a new generation can live on. Essentially, interrupting this process equals higher yields.

The following list of suggested fruits and vegetables to grow in an apartment garden is not utterly inclusive, but it is a solid guide for both beginners and people who really want to produce as much as they can in a small amount of space. These plants were chosen for one or more of several key characteristics that make them worthwhile—ease, taste, or high yields.

Arugula

Arugula is a bitter salad green. A member of the Brassicaceae or mustard family, arugula is considered a cold-weather crop and does well in the cooler temperatures of early spring and fall. People often ask me why their arugula didn't do well; more often than not, it's because they waited too long to sow seeds and the weather was already too warm. Arugula is a leafy green that produces long flat leaves with a distinct peppery flavor. Each seed produces one thin stem, which leaves grow out from. You can further your harvest by cutting them back often—leaves will regenerate once and maybe even twice before getting too spicy, woody, or bitter.

Where and When to Plant

Sow arugula seeds in the top layer of potting soil in March or April. Sow again in late summer and early fall—late August and anytime through October.

Pot Size

If given the room, arugula plants may grow to well over two feet. In a small to medium container, however, leaves grow to the perfect size for salad.

How to Harvest

Cut arugula at the base of each leaf off the main stem. You can decide for yourself when the leaf is big enough. For a mellow, spicy flavor and a tender green, harvest when leaves are young—about three to four inches. If you prefer a stronger flavor and a thicker, crunchier stem, allow them to grow to five to six inches and cut the entire stem at its base. Arugula bolts (goes to flower) quickly in the heat. If this happens, strip the woody stem of its leaves and use both the leaves and flowers in your salads. Woody stems can be chopped finely and used to make a *gremolata* (a chopped herb condiment) or as stuffing for savory dishes.

Cucumber

Cucumbers do well in containers because individual vines are prolific and will produce a decent amount of fruit even when given a small space. Growing in a large container will provide enough fruit to make any effort worthwhile. (Although ideally they should be grown in the ground, as their taproots will run down as far as two feet if given the chance.)

Choose small varieties, as they will mature fairly quickly. Cornichons, gherkins, and other pickling cucumbers do better in containers than the larger slicing varieties.

Where and When to Plant

Plant out cucumbers throughout June in the Pacific Northwest (earlier in warmer climates). They don't take super well to transplanting, but you can try starting them indoors in early May for a jump on the season.

Pot Size

Use a large pot for cucumbers, and sow four seeds per pot at the farthest corners from each other. A cucumber's side roots, much like zucchini's, tend to branch out widely in just the first few inches of soil layer, so a wide square pot offers the best space. Thin out any small vines after six weeks to allow the more prolific vines space to grow.

How to Harvest

Snap cucumbers from the stem when they are ready, or use a flat knife to cut them off just above where the stem connects to the fruit. Small varieties are best harvested when they are just that—small. Don't try to grow them larger, as they turn bitter and the seed membrane becomes weblike and unpalatable.

Lettuce

Whether you opt for butterhead, romaine, crisphead, or loose-leaf, lettuce is one of the quickest and easiest plants to grow. Little Gem (a romaine variety), Rouge d'Hiver (a cross between romaine and butterhead), and Oak Leaf (a loose-leaf lettuce) are all great choices. If you'd like a summer lettuce, be sure to choose a heat-tolerant variety. If you know you'll be planting in fall, a cool-season lettuce is in order. For flexibility, purchase a variety of lettuce types at the beginning of the year and sow according to the season.

Where and When to Plant

Lettuce can be sown almost any time of year, depending on your climate, so it's best to read the back of the seed packets to determine the timing that is best for each type.

Pot Size

Sow seeds in a long, shallow, pale-colored plastic container, since lettuces are shallow-rooted, and plastic containers hold water a bit longer than clay ones. Smaller pots tend to heat up faster than a large deep pot, so choosing a light color helps keep the roots cool, as well. Be sure to keep the seedbed moist until seeds germinate, which typically happens in five to seven days.

How to Harvest

To harvest lettuce, try to remove the larger outer leaves first. Using a small pair of scissors, cut the individual leaf stems as close to the base of the main stem as possible, leaving some interior leaves behind. These leaves will soon fill in and become outer leaves; thus you're creating a cycle of lettuce leaves to harvest. If you prefer to harvest complete heads of lettuce, do so when the heads are full and the outer leaves are starting to yellow and wilt, but know that if you cut the entire plant, the odds of its regenerating are reduced.

Miner's Lettuce

Miner's lettuce is a succulent green that is also a native, mountainous plant and can be both cultivated and found in the wild. It may also go by the name purslane or claytonia. Stems branch out from the plant's base and can be cut and eaten in salads. This plant prefers cool, damp conditions, so it's great for a balcony that receives only partial sun. This green adds a nice bright lime color to salads and has a characteristic slightly sour lemon flavor, not unlike sorrel. The small white flowers can be eaten, as well. It's a great addition to a salad garden because of its early sow date, preference for shade, and unique flavor.

Where and When to Plant

Plant miner's lettuce out in early spring. You can seed directly into pots from February through early April, and again in fall. Miner's lettuce does not like heat.

Pot Size

A shallow-rooted plant, miner's lettuce does well in small shallow containers. As it has a pronounced flavor, a little goes a long way. Choose a container that is five inches deep and about as wide. You can grow more greens in a longer rectangular container. I find that a twelve-inch-long container will produce plenty of extra salad greens for two people over the course of a season.

How to Harvest

As with most greens, cut miner's lettuce leaves at the base of its stem, leaving the main stem intact. The plant will regenerate a few times before turning red-brown and dying back.

Snap Pea

Snap peas are one of the earliest seeds you can sow in
the spring, especially if you're using a container, as
you don't need to wait for soil to dry up after winter
rains. Peas have root systems that spread laterally but
don't grow down too deep and are therefore great for
containers. They also put up pretty sweet pea flowers
(that then turn into peas) and grow tall, adding some
height to the garden. In addition to pea pods, you can
also harvest pea vines from the plant without hurting
production too much. Clip new vine growth and use in
sautés or soups.

Where and When to Plant

Sow pea seeds directly into your pot in early spring—from around
the middle of March to the beginning of April—and cover with an
inch of soil. Keep the seedbed well watered so the buried seeds
stay moist until germination.

Pot Size

Plant in a large, wide, deep pot. Choose the largest terra-cotta or
plastic pot you can find. The standard large pot is about eighteen
inches deep and about that wide.

How to Harvest

Snap the peas from the vine when the pods are full and firm, and
be sure to keep the plant harvested. If you leave mature pea pods
on the vine, the plant will stop producing altogether (convinced
that its work is done for the season), and the pea pods will become
chewy and thick.

Strawberry

Strawberries are fun to grow because a single plant can tolerate the
confinement of a small pot, and they are pretty plants as well. They
are one of the first plants to come up in spring, and when the weather
really warms up, small fruits form to announce summer's arrival. If

you hope to harvest bowl after bowl of strawberries, you should really try to find a big patch to grow them in. But if you don't mind a small bowl every year, and you're in it just for the thrill, a plant or two will do.

Where and When to Plant

Strawberries can be set out first thing in spring. Purchase starts rather than trying to grow from seed or (if you have access to a strawberry patch) clip a runner and plant that. In fall, be sure to mulch the pot completely so the plants are protected and will survive the winter. I've had the same strawberry plants for four years now and don't invest much time in them other than watering and mulching.

Pot Size

One strawberry plant will fit in a small pot that is at least six inches deep. In a good, hot year you'll harvest four or five strawberries from the plant. If you'd like more, try starting with one plant in a long narrow pot. The plant will send out runners that will eventually grow into full plants.

How to Harvest

You know how to harvest strawberries! Just pick them off the stem. When they are ripe and ready, they will fall off easily into your hand.

Zucchini

Zucchini and other summer squashes are the plants that keep on giving. Squashes are prolific, and you don't need many to keep you in a productive crop most of the summer. Zucchini can be harvested when small or left alone to get big and fat. Just remember that the longer you leave the squash on a plant, the less the plant will produce, and the bigger the seeds and the seed membranes will become.

Where and When to Plant

Zucchini and summer squashes follow the same rules as cucumbers. (Incidentally, squashes and cucumbers come from the same plant family, so they have similar planting needs.) Sow zucchini in early June or late May if the temperatures are consistently in the 60s. You can also sow in late June or even early July for a late-season crop, but if it is a cool summer, this may not work.

Pot Size

Use a large pot for zucchini, and sow four seeds per pot at the farthest corners from each other. Zucchini roots spread out shallowly. They tend to be fat and fleshy for about seven or eight inches of depth, then fan out into root hairs. For this reason they are well suited to container growing. Thin any vines that are being dwarfed after six weeks.

How to Harvest

Snap zucchini straight from the stem, or cut using a straight-edged knife. You can harvest zucchini when they are young or wait until they are older and riper. Younger squashes are quite firm and will hold their shape in sautés or on the grill. A more mature fruit has a softer flesh and larger seeds. It is a personal preference for when best to harvest.

Herbs

Herbs are champions in the apartment garden: no matter how much you harvest, they keep on giving. Herbs are fairly easy to grow; they require varying pot sizes, depending on their root systems. Many herbs are perennials, so they return year after year, signaling spring's arrival. You can overwinter perennial herbs in their pots. Most will come back in spring even when neglected over winter—a great choice for the lazy gardener.

Herbs are potent little plants, and your kitchen will never feel lacking with bunches of fresh stems and branches on hand. Herbs may be dried or infused to extend their life outside of the garden. For the apartment garden, herbs are the quintessential low-maintenance, high-reward plants to grow.

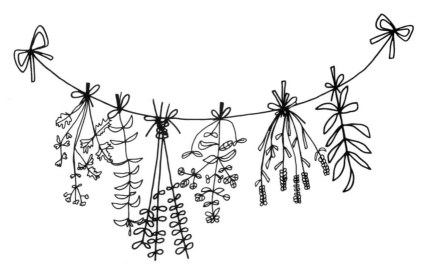

Anise Hyssop

The unique flavor of anise hyssop is part licorice, part mint, a little bit like honey—herbal perfection. It is nice in grain salads and as a digestive tea or tisane after a big meal or between courses. This herb is best grown from seed. Recently, I've seen anise hyssop starts at the nursery, but don't count on finding them easily. The plant grows tall, sturdy stalks topped with vibrant purple flowers. Anise hyssop is a perennial and will come back year after year.

QUICK LIST OF PERENNIALS

Perennials are plants that live for longer than two years in succession. For apartment and container gardens, this applies mostly to herbaceous plants. These plants grow in spring, flower in summer, and go dormant in winter. The following year they put on growth again from the same rootstock, as well as distributing seed as annuals do. For this reason, perennials can often be divided and shared with fellow gardeners.

Perennials are awesome to have in your garden, as they generally need less attention than annuals do and are fairly hardy. In temperate climates, like the Pacific Northwest, most perennials will survive outside over winter, even without extra mulching. An added benefit, as small apartments typically don't have extra room to bring all those pots indoors! If you live in a region with hard frosts, it is best to move your perennials under some form of protection. A cellar or unheated garage will work well. For areas with mild winters, plan to prepare perennial pots with a thick layer of mulch, then wait the winter out and hope for the best. On my own patio, there have been really cold years in which I've lost geraniums, lovage, and scented sages, but they are easily replaced come spring.

When planting for the first time, be sure to give these plants plenty of space to stretch their roots and grow, as you will have them in your garden for longer than a year. The bigger the pot, the more herb you'll have to harvest, so select your favorites and give them some space.

Following is a quick list of perennial herbs to consider when you're starting your apartment garden.

Chives	Oregano
Dill	Rosemary
Lemon Balm	Sage
Lovage	Thyme
Mint	

Where and When to Plant

Anise hyssop can be sown in spring, directly in a pot. The seeds are super tiny and need only be pressed into the soil. Because the seeds are so light and small, anise hyssop tends to spread seed liberally after it flowers. Expect it to crop up in other pots the following year. I let these stray seeds grow to small seedlings before I repot them or give them away to friends. Anise hyssop likes sun but will do well in partial shade with at least six to eight hours of sunlight.

Pot Size

Anise hyssop appreciates some room to grow, so select a deep pot. Flower stalks may reach over two feet tall, and the extra depth helps the plant to grow high. Shoot for a two-foot depth and about that much width on a pot.

How to Harvest

Cut off an entire stalk just above a leaf line. When the plant flowers, cut back the entire main stem, as it may regenerate growth.

Chervil

Chervil is one of my very favorite herbs. With tender fernlike leaves, it is extremely dainty and delicate. The flavor is not unlike dill, but it is sharper and more crisp. It doesn't linger on your palate as dill can, and it won't overpower a dish. Chervil is a great match for eggs, light broths, and white fish of any kind.

Where and When to Plant

Chervil can be sown from seed in early spring well before many other plants, or in late summer for a second crop. Depending on the geographic climate, plants sown in February or March often flower and reseed themselves when the temperatures are just right. Chervil does well in partial shade; in fact, if it gets too warm, it will bolt quickly.

Pot Size

Chervil can be grown in a medium-depth pot, about eight to twelve inches deep. The wider the pot, the more the plant will fill in, so keep that in mind when choosing.

How to Harvest

Cut the entire stem of chervil and use both leaves and stem. The plant will quickly fill back in.

Chives

Chives do well in containers, look beautiful, are quite flavorful, and come back year after year. This plant sends up thin hollow stalks tasting strongly of onion. When chives blossom (typically in late May or early June), the flower heads are equally flavorful and can be used in salads and dressings of any kind. After flowering, cut back the entire plant to about 1 inch; it will grow and flower again later in summer.

Where and When to Plant

Chives can be sown from seed early in April. They are prolific and grow quickly, so I recommend purchasing seeds instead of starts, or take a small clump from a friend's garden. Chives will readily reseed if given the opportunity, so be diligent about deadheading the spent blossoms, which contain the seed.

Pot Size

A medium-sized pot is usually plenty for a steady supply of chives from spring through summer. Pick a pot that is at least twelve inches deep and about that wide.

How to Harvest

Cut chive stems close to the base of the plant, leaving about an inch of green. The plant will fill back in. Start from the outside of the plant and work your way in as new growth develops. When the plant flowers, pick off the entire flower head and crumble to separate the purple blossoms to use in recipes.

Lemon Balm

Like cilantro, lemon balm is a polarizing herb: most either love it or hate it. Lemon balm has the tenacity to grow even in the worst conditions. Because of this, I recommend it for the absolute garden novice. You can neglect lemon balm all year, and it will come back the following year with only a small amount of attention. The flavorful leaves are strong enough that they can be considered soapy. Lemon balm makes a great quick tea, especially when combined with mint or anise hyssop.

Where and When to Plant

Lemon balm can be planted in early spring. As a member of the mint family, it can tolerate some shade. Lemon balm will also spread quickly, if given the opportunity, so it's a plant best kept in a container. It is thought to have medicinal properties; for a digestive tea, steep in hot water and sweeten with honey. It's also a great complement to snap peas, which come in at the same time in spring.

Pot Size

A medium-sized pot—eight to twelve inches deep and about just as wide—will be ample for lemon balm, as it's hardy and you will not use it often. When the plant fills the pot, you can easily divide it (pop it out of the pot and split the plant and root in two) and start a second pot if you so desire.

How to Harvest

Cut entire stems from the plant, making sure to cut just above the first set of leaves. Use the smaller, more tender leaves for recipes, as the older, larger leaves may be tough. Try both and see which you prefer—you may just prefer that big flavor.

Lemon Verbena

Growing lemon verbena is not entirely practical for the apartment gardener; because it is a tender perennial, you have to closely monitor its condition. You need to nurture lemon verbena by taking it indoors to overwinter. But with that extra effort comes a handsome reward. Lemon verbena is a beautiful plant to grow, with slender, twig-like branches and long, rippled, glossy leaves that are delicate and stunning. There is truly nothing like lemon verbena—its flavor is both floral and lemony. Try lemon verbena in beverages and infused into sugar. It also makes an interesting addition (in small amounts) to a green salad, and is fabulous when mashed up into a *gremolata* to accompany lamb.

Where and When to Plant

Purchase a start for lemon verbena in late spring—no sooner than May. Verbena likes hot conditions, so it's best to set the plant in full sun and be sure to keep it watered regularly.

Pot Size

A large pot will allow for a large shrub with many branches and leaves. Choose a container at least two feet deep and about as wide so the lemon verbena can grow big and tall.

How to Harvest

Cut off entire branches from the plant; steer clear of the main stem and cut just above a set of leaves. It will regrow.

Lovage

Lovage looks and tastes like celery with a more pronounced flavor. The leaves are a bit bigger and can be chopped into salads, soups, and seafood dishes. Lovage is a perennial that will come back year after year and can withstand some neglect. I stuck some lovage root in a pot over three years ago, and except for some watering and pruning back in fall, I haven't done a thing to help it along. Lovage may flower and seed if you give it enough room to grow. I keep lovage in a medium-sized pot, and it has flowered only once. On bigger plants, you can collect the seed in late summer and used it to stock your pantry. Ground up, the seed can be used as a spice rub on meat or fish, or even used as an addition to cinnamon in fruit pies and crisps.

Where and When to Plant

Lovage can be planted from rootstock in fall—ask a friend to cut you a small portion. Place in a large pot of soil, water, and mulch with dry leaves for insulation over the winter. If you don't have a cutting, in early spring purchase a start and plant it directly into your pot.

Pot Size

With this herb, the bigger the pot, the bigger the plant. A medium-large-sized pot about a foot deep and about as wide will produce enough to use occasionally throughout the year. If you have the space for a larger pot, though, I highly recommend it. This plant will grow very tall and wide if you let it, and it's an absolute marvel to see in a garden.

How to Harvest

Cut lovage at the base of the stems, working from the outside of the plant in. Big outer stems can often be quite strong in flavor, so make sure to harvest smaller tender stalks often. The plant will continue to produce through summer.

Marjoram

Marjoram is a strong-flavored herb, very similar to oregano, but with a softer note. It can be added raw to dishes, but will also withstand some heat from cooking. Try it in tomato sauces and gravies or as a small addition to salads. Marjoram is a perennial herb, though it can be tender, and you will often see it sold as an annual. It's a great herb for drying.

Where and When to Plant

Sow marjoram directly into pots in April, or purchase a start and plant out. Better yet, start seeds inside in March. They grow quickly and will take off once it's warm enough to set them outside in late spring.

Pot Size

A medium-sized pot will suffice for marjoram. Pick a pot a bit deeper than six inches with a wide opening.

How to Harvest

You can harvest whole stems of marjoram by cutting at the base of the stem. Once the plant flowers, cut back about half way and it will put on new growth quickly.

Mint

Mint is a fabulous herb to perk up grain salads, crush into a pesto for roasted meats, or add to a fizzy summertime beverage. Mint is a considered a "runner"—a plant that sends out horizontal root runners that produce new stalks. Choose a long, shallow pot to allow it room to spread. Most garden centers carry transplants of mint, or you can ask a neighbor for a clipping. Mint is prolific and will establish itself quickly. It is also a great herb to dry and save for tisanes.

Where and When to Plant

Mint can be planted out nearly all year long. Plant mint in the spring through early summer or fall in most areas. Plant in full to partial sun and keep the soil moist. Mint does not like wet feet, so be mindful that the soil drains well and do not let water stand in the drainage saucer after watering.

Pot Size

For a continuous supply of mint, choose a medium-sized pot, at least ten inches deep and nine inches wide.

How to Harvest

Cut entire stems from the mint plant, at their base, as close to the soil as possible.

Thyme

Thyme is one of the most versatile herbs to cook with. It is easy to grow and will come back year after year. Thyme is indispensable in stocks or for roasting meats, but it can also be used in sweet desserts and pairs well with fruit such as plums and blueberries. Be sure to select a culinary thyme (English thyme is a favorite), as there are many members in the thyme family and not all of them taste great. If you purchase a start, taste a leave first to see if you like the flavor. Scented thymes are interesting additions to the garden. Lemon thyme has a distinctive citrus aroma and can be used in most recipes that call for English thyme.

Where and When to Plant

Thyme is a hardy herb, adaptable to various weather conditions. You can plant in spring, summer, or fall with good results. Thyme does well in dappled shade and does not need full sun to be vigorous.

Pot Size

Thyme has a shallow root system but will spread if you give it space to branch out. Grow thyme in a wide, shallow pot or even a wooden flat or box.

How to Harvest

Choose whole branches of thyme and cut them at the base, just above a set of leaves. You should also cut back your thyme in early summer after it blooms (generally in June), as it will fill in and provide tender bushy growth all summer and through fall.

Flowers

Flowers are a beautiful addition to any garden. Thin stems blowing in the breeze and topped with bright colored petals add life and texture to the garden. Not only are flowers visually stunning, but they also attract pollinators to the garden. Bees, insects, and birds fly from plant to plant, eating nectar and spreading pollen. This cross-pollination is crucial for some plants to fruit or flower, therefore, flowers are an important part of a healthy garden ecosystem. Luckily, some flowers play a role in our kitchens as well. Petals are often edible—though few have a distinctive flavor, they add eye appeal with their delicate forms and color—and some leaves of flowering plants can be used in salads and cocktails. Many plants also produce edible seeds that can be used as garnish on dishes or dried and kept for winter pantry-stocking. Get creative and use blossoms in teas and infusions, try chopping stems into salads, or use leaves as part of your table setting.

Many flowers will reseed themselves if given the opportunity, so be prepared to either *deadhead* plants (remove all the dead, dry flower heads that hold the seeds) and save the seed, or allow them to spread among your containers. It's pretty cool to let flowers drop seed and see where they crop up the following year. I have grown anise hyssop in one pot, only to have new anise hyssop plants sprout up across the deck in a pot ten feet away the following year. It's pretty amazing that a little seed can travel so far, land on a small surface of soil, survive the winter, and create a new plant.

Borage

These tall, prickly-stemmed plants are not only a gorgeous addition to a small garden, but also a tasty one. Borage grows two to three feet tall on a sturdy stalk that sends out sparse but large, hairy, edible leaves. Harvest young leaves for the best flavor—the spiky hairs on mature leaves can turn some people off. The leaves have a slight cucumber flavor, great for a Pimm's Cup cocktail. Flowers blossom and turn a deep purple-blue and can be used as an edible garnish. This plant attracts pollinators to the garden and is therefore a great plant to grow alongside fruiting vegetables.

Where and When to Plant

Plant borage seeds in late spring or early summer, sometime between May and June, as this plant needs warmer soil temperatures to germinate.

Pot Size

Plant borage in a deep pot. When given plenty of space for the roots to branch out, the plant can grow to maturity, which is when it is most stunning. Sow four to six seeds directly into the potting soil; if all germinate, you will need to thin them, leaving the two or three strongest seedlings in the container.

How to Harvest

Harvest borage leaves by pulling or clipping new small leaves from the main stem. Harvest flowers when the petals fully open and they turn deep blue.

Chamomile

Chamomile is a wispy-stemmed plant with small white flowers that looks like a daisy. The plants have a distinctive sweet-floral scent, and flower buds can be used in teas or sweet recipes. Chamomile comes in many varieties, but the self-seeding annual German chamomile is the common plant for teas and infusions. If you are growing chamomile in the ground and do not wish it to spread, be sure to deadhead.

Where and When to Plant

Chamomile prefers full sun and should be planted in late spring, once temperatures have warmed and remain consistent. Because chamomile is such a delicate stem, it makes for a great border plant. Try planting a start close to the container's edge, and allow the stems to droop over. One chamomile start would fit nicely in a large container planted with borage.

Pot Size

German chamomile grows low to the ground and spreads, with a shallow root system. Try tucking this plant into a small pot—six inches deep and at least that wide at the rim. The larger the pot, the larger the harvest will be.

How to Harvest

Pop full flower heads off the plant for use in recipes. You can use them fresh or place them in a single layer on a drying rack. Once dry, they can be stored in a small spice jar in your pantry.

Lavender

Lavender is both a pretty and useful flower to grow. We tend to think of lavender as a cutting flower or a cosmetic or medicinal herb, but it is also edible, and its blossoms can be used in a number of ways in the kitchen. Small amounts will gently perfume savory dishes like goat cheese, lamb, or duck. The flowers may also be used in sweet recipes. I prefer it in syrups, used to brush the tops of cakes for a subtle floral essence, or as a refreshing cocktail accompaniment. Lavender is a heat lover and will do best with a west-facing deck or balcony, where the sun is strongest. Select English lavender for a culinary variety. Other lavenders are technically edible, but English has a sweet and pleasant perfume that is most suitable for cooking.

Where and When to Plant

Purchase lavender starts in the spring and set them out in a spot with full sun. Lavender plants prefer the heat and prosper in warm, arid conditions.

Pot Size

The pot size for your lavender should be determined by how big you'd like the plant to grow. A large pot will allow for room to grow for two years or more. A too small pot will require transplanting in the second year. At a minimum, start with a medium-sized pot, about twelve inches deep and about that wide.

How to Harvest

Cut lavender stems just above the foliage and use the blossoms only. Cutting this way may produce a second bloom. Lavender dries well, and when dry the flavor is more pronounced. Once the flowers start to die back, cut back the entire plant down to the leaves. It may produce a second blooming late in the season.

Nasturtium

Nasturtiums are long vining plants that do well in poor soil. They prefer full sun but tolerate some shade. Make sure your space offers nasturtiums at least six hours of direct sun. Their propensity to put on growth no matter the level of neglect makes them great for patio farmers who may not be successful with more demanding flowers. All parts of the nasturtium are edible: they are grown chiefly for their edible flowers and young seed buds, but the vines are also quite tender and succulent. Flower heads can be picked and tossed in salad for color or lightly sugared and used as garnish for a dessert. Young seeds that are still light green and immature can be harvested and pickled in vinegar like capers (see Chapter 6, Recipes from the Garden, for a recipe). I often use the pretty lily-pad-like leaves for coasters on the dinner table. They are delicately veined and add that fresh-from-the-garden vibe to your meals.

Where and When to Plant

Plant nasturtiums at the same time you sow cucumbers, in early June. Make sure you tuck them into a pot that will allow them to vine out without blocking too much sun from other plants. You can start them earlier indoors in seed trays, but these flowers grow quickly, so you won't necessarily notice a difference.

Pot Size

Choose a medium-sized pot for these flowers. The root systems do not run very deep, and they may quickly crowd your space, which can happen if you give the roots too much room. Plant about three seeds per container in the shape of a triangle and keep the seedbed moist until they germinate.

How to Harvest

Pick flower heads, seeds, or leaves directly from the plant. It should go without saying that if you harvest all the flowers from the plant, it cannot produce seeds—so if you're growing nasturtium strictly to harvest seeds for pickling, you should leave most flowers on the plant.

Nigella

Nigella is more commonly known as love-in-a-mist, and several plant species go by the name. For culinary use, choose *Nigella sativa*, also known as black cumin or onion seed. Cornflower blue, sharply triangular flowers sit on a thin stem with wispy fronds that look like fennel. Once the blooms fade, thin-skinned paper-lantern-like seedpods develop. Some people use the dried pods in floral arrangements, but the seeds are edible and can be used as garnish, just like poppy seeds.

Where and When to Plant

Nigella should be directly sown in spring, with successive sowings through early summer. This plant likes sun but does not need constant exposure. A pot with morning sun works well. Nigella is a self-seeding annual.

Pot Size

For a splash of color and good production of seeds, give nigella lots of room to grow. Choose a deep pot—at least eighteen inches. The width of the pot is not as important, as nigella grows tall and the roots do not spread wide.

How to Harvest

Leave the flowers to form seedpods. When the seedpods have dried and turned brown, pull off the heads and shake out the seeds. Store the seeds in a glass spice container in your spice cupboard.

Scented Geraniums

Scented geranium leaves come in varying hues of green or have variegated leaves, which are heavily perfumed and can be harvested to use in sweet recipes. Geraniums come back each year (unless it's a really cold winter with several freezes) and will survive warm weather with blatant neglect. Many flower in varying shades of pink and white, but it's the foliage that holds the oil. To decide which geranium to purchase, rub a leaf gently between your thumb and index finger to pick up some of the plant's natural oil, then smell it to see whether or not you like the scent. Scented geraniums come in a wide range of aromas—mint, nutmeg, rose, lemon, and many others.

Where and When to Plant

Geraniums do well in dappled sun or partly shady spaces, so long as they get *some* sunlight. They can be planted nearly any time of the year. If you have winters with long freezes, move the plants inside until spring.

Pot Size

You can use smaller pots for geraniums, as you likely won't use much in recipes. A few leaves a year will keep you well stocked. Choose a pot at least eight inches deep. If you would like the plant to grow larger the following year, transplant it to a larger pot in the fall.

How to Harvest

Most plants do best when you harvest whole stems. In the case of scented geraniums, however, a little goes a long way, so I sometimes choose big juicy leaves and pluck them from the main stem of the plant. If using several leaves, cut an entire stem from the plant, just above a leaf line.

Shungiku Edible Chrysanthemum

The first time I tasted this chrysanthemum from one of my gardens, I was floored by the flavor. It is a common Asian green, often used in stir-fries. Chrysanthemum greens are citrusy and sharp, with a mellow herbaceous finish. They taste *so* good! The leaves are long, slim, and softly fringed, and make a beautiful garnish. You can use the leaves in salads or muddled into summer cocktails. The flower heads can be dried and used as a tea.

Where and When to Plant

Sow chrysanthemum directly into pots in April and all the way through early summer. Some people find the flavor of the mature leaves (from a plant that has flowered) too strong. Try it and decide for yourself; you can plant a second sowing if you want a continuous harvest.

Pot Size

I like to seed chrysanthemums in a deep container so they can grow tall and long. You can also grow a dozen plants in a wide container. Opt for a box at least eighteen inches deep and about that wide.

How to Harvest

Cut entire stems from the plant and pick off the leaves.

Honeybees

I love bees—in particular, honeybees. Bees act as pollinators, a crucial role in producing fruit in your garden. They are incredibly loyal to their queen and live to work for her, supplying the hive with pollen for honey. Watching honeybees is a rewarding way to spend an hour—get out there, find a hive, and watch the magic happen.

Honeybees are an excellent addition to any garden, and they work particularly well in a small space because they take up so little room. Additionally, honeybees will travel a few miles to collect nectar to turn to honey for the hive, so you need not have an overly active garden in order to support them. I have long wanted to keep a stack of honeybee boxes on my apartment deck, but my neighbor is opposed to the idea.

Honeybees make honey with nectar they collect from local flowers that are in bloom. Depending on what pollen is collected, the flavor of the honey can vary widely from hive to hive. Bees start working in spring, as the weather warms and the days grow longer. As flowers bloom, honeybees fly from blossom to blossom and grab tiny drops of nectar, returning them to the hive where they are then converted to honey by the worker bees. The bees survive off this honey. Quite simply, they work in the warm months to gather and store enough honey to feed them through the winter. This process is easily observed by setting up camp near a hive or sitting still in a garden. Bees can be incredibly single-minded—when they're working, they have little interest in anything else other than work. As long as you steer clear of the bee line, honeybees seldom sting.

One particular bonus of beekeeping, other than their stellar garden powers and honey production, is their limited demands. Honeybees need warmth and sun, so the hive should be located in a light space with good daily sun exposure. Other than that, they need only a little bit of space to do their job. An urbanite with a decent-sized deck or balcony can keep honeybees. Some equipment is needed, but it is not prohibitively expensive, nor does it take up much space. A beekeeping suit is never a bad idea (though some people are com-

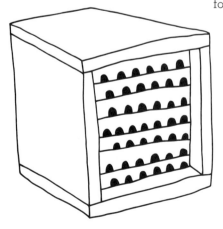

fortable with only a protective hat and netting), and a smoker helps to keep bees docile. Of course, you also need to invest in the hive.

Cultivated bee hives are made of stacked boxes for the bees to work in. Inside each box are a number of frames. The frames fit into the box and are lined with beeswax.

Bees build cells on these frames and fill them with honey. Honeycomb frames can be removed midseason for honey harvesting. This can be done simply by positioning a frame over a large stainless steel bowl and allowing the honey to drip in. You may also invest in an electric honey extractor—hand-cranked varieties work well and are less expensive. Honey can be bottled in clean jars and used all year long.

As a beekeeper, you have to decide how much honey to take and how much to leave for the hive's food store. Bees will do their job with or without your help, so you have to learn to adapt yourself to their life cycle. When there are lots of blooming trees and plants, the bees will be active, so you will be active. As blooms die back, so will their daily work. A beekeeper also has to keep an eye on the health of the hive, watching out for mites and disease. In the high season, plan on looking into your hive once a week.

As the season progresses, bees continue to work with a focus on building up winter stores. The honey they produce in season will feed them all winter. Most bees spend winter in a hibernation state. They cluster up with the queen in the middle of the hive and move through the frames at a slow rate, eating the honey stored in summer. In winter the beekeeper need only check on the hive occasionally to make sure there is enough honey for the bees and supplement only as necessary.

While beekeeping has to be timely, it does not need to take a huge amount of time. Bees are less demanding than most household pets, though they need a watchful eye over the long term. In recent years, bee populations have declined and continue to struggle. Urban beekeeping should be considered as a small-scale antidote. It goes without saying that keeping bees also connects individuals to nature and the seasons—an important part of life that many are rediscovering. The resulting fruit of your labor—honey—is one that shouldn't go unnoted. Honey is nutritious and has enzymes and trace minerals along with medicinal properties. It is an antibiotic and has healing properties, as well.

Most cities and counties have extension programs with educational offerings for beekeeping. They are a great place to start and gather information about hives, equipment, and the bees themselves. As with any big project, it is always best to do some personal exploring before taking the leap. Dig around and see what you come up with. When all is said and done, I hope you find honey dripping down your fingers some summer day real soon.

Chapter 4

Seeds, Seed Starting & Propagation

Seeds

Searching for and choosing which seeds to grow is definitely one of the best parts of gardening. There is something powerful about a seed packet full of possibility. It does not seem likely that one small seed could produce enough food to put on your table, but it will. To have a hand in the process is nothing short of fascinating. The first time I planted a vegetable garden, I was surprised and awestruck that the plants actually sprouted and continued to grow. Seeing lettuces, leeks, and other small green stems poke out of the rich, dark soil for the first time was thrilling.

There are so many seed sources, from the nursery to the hardware store to mail order and online companies, that it can be challenging to choose the right seeds. As a general rule of thumb, always purchase organic seed. Several companies sell

only organic seed that can be ordered online (check out the Resources section on page 175). By purchasing organic seed, you are supporting growers who have carefully bred seed for the best production. It is best to choose varieties adapted to your local conditions whenever possible. Plants evolve and change to accommodate their environment, so when you purchase seed that has been grown close to home (or grown in conditions similar to where you live), you're increasing your chances of success. Additionally, as big corporations continue to gain control over the vast majority of our seed options, purchasing organic helps keep diversity alive. Over the last several hundred years, we have lost a fair amount of genetic diversity in our seeds; as gardeners, we have the ability to play a key role in that diversity. Organic seed, particularly from open-pollinated and heirloom varieties (more on this shortly), can also be harvested, saved, and replanted.

Seed saving is an awesome process to observe and a great way to adapt seeds to your own microclimate. Over time, you have the ability to condition your seeds to do well in your personal garden space. Saving your own seed is not only an engrossing project, but it will also better help you to understand the life cycle of a plant. And it's economical too!

When choosing seeds, be mindful of sow dates and maturing times. Many seed packets say "Sow after last frost," which is a vague time frame that can be confusing. In my view, seeds fall into three basic categories of planting times: those that can be planted first thing in spring, those that do well in heat (considered "heat tolerant"), and those that are good for cool-weather crops. For more specific information, it's best to consult a local planting calendar first and not try to deduce what to plant when based solely on the packet. Maturing times ("50 days," "85 days") will give you a good frame of reference for the life cycle of your plant. These are helpful, as they allow you to plan your garden around your schedule and make plans based on when you will be harvesting. For example, if you're planting lettuce in May and traveling for the month of July, you should steer clear of varieties with a 60-day maturing time.

Seed packets will also note whether the plant is open-pollinated, heirloom, or hybrid. Open-pollinated and heirloom seeds produce mature plants that create seeds that, when replanted, stay true to the parent plant. Opt for these varieties if you would like to save your seed. Hybrid plants have been cross-bred in some way, and if you save the seed, they will not produce plants with the same qualities as the parent plant.

Because you are growing in small containers that essentially limit a plant's size, it is best to choose a smaller variety of plant, when available. If dwarf varieties of your favorite vegetable are available, select those. It is also important to keep the climate in mind when purchasing seeds. For example, the Pacific Northwest has a short, cool summer season but mild winters, which allow year-round gardening of hardy greens and brassicas. Large melons, peppers, and corn are challenging to grow here. In contrast, Midwestern states have a long, hot summer season, ideal for tomatoes and peppers, but winters are generally too cold for unprotected outdoor crops. Be sure to follow the list of edible plants from Chapter 3, What to Grow, For Real. Start with those nearly foolproof basics and branch out in later years as you become more familiar with the practice of growing.

Seed Starting

I used to think starting plants from seed was a project best left to nurseries. My vision of small plants coming to life included rows and rows of seed trays set within the confines of the hot and steamy glass walls of a greenhouse. The process of seed starting always seemed elusive to me—even a little bit confusing. In truth, it is very easy to start your own seeds at home.

In the Pacific Northwest, where I tend gardens, in early spring it stays moist and cool, and our days are short. These conditions hinder germination of seeds. We have to wait for the ground to dry up and the sun to start shining to really take full advantage of the garden. The same goes for New England, though they have to wait for the ground to thaw. By stark comparison, gardeners in California can garden year-round. In every condition, however, starting seeds at home accelerates the process of growing.

There are clear benefits to seed starting. Starting seeds indoors will extend your growing season. When you start seeds in advance of their sow dates, you get a jump on the season. Instead of planting out seed directly in your garden, you plant an actual plant! This extra time means you'll be harvesting earlier. More importantly for home gardeners, though, starting your own seeds opens up a world of crops to you. Relying on nurseries and farmers to supply your plant starts means you get to choose only from what they decide to grow. Choosing your own varieties of vegetable from pages of colorful catalogs is much more satisfying. You can experiment with varieties that are not well known and try something new. I always think, why bother

MAKING YOUR OWN SEED-STARTING MIX

Seed-starting mix provides a sterile environment (seeds do not need nutrients during their early growth stage) and allows for air and moisture to pass easily through the growing medium. You can purchase commercial seed-starting mix, but the bags are often too big for the small amount needed. Years ago I started mixing my own, and it works just as well. Making up small batches spares you from needing much storage space and is much less expensive.

What You'll Need

3 parts coco coir

1 part perlite

¹/₂ part pumice

What to Do

The coco coir is a nice fluffy fibrous ingredient that allows air and water to circulate around the seedlings. Perlite and pumice are both derived from volcanic rock and also help with drainage and air circulation. In a deep bucket or large plastic bag, soak the brick of coco coir in one or two cups of water to moisten and reconstitute it. Add water as needed, aiming to make the coco coir moist, but not wet. When ready, measure the coco coir parts and add appropriate amounts of perlite and pumice. Stir thoroughly. Use it immediately for starting seeds. Any extra mix should be left to dry out somewhat, then stored until it is ready to use. At that time, add water to remoisten.

growing varieties that everyone else will grow? I seek out something new every year. Additionally, it is more economical to buy seeds. One pack of lettuce seeds will have you in salad for the length of a season and costs about the same as one four-inch pot of starts.

Many beginners trust that a sunny windowsill will receive enough light to grow plants. This is not always true. Southwest-facing windows will have the most exposure to sun, assuming your view is unobstructed and light flows freely in. Even then, depending on your latitude, in the dead of winter the sun is not out long enough to supply adequate light. Most apartments, therefore, don't have the perfect growing conditions and will need some supplies to mimic them.

Plants need light, warmth, moisture, and root nourishment to grow. Seeds can be started in ordinary indoor light, but once they push up out of the soil, the seedlings need up to twelve hours of light daily to grow vigorously. In the northern hemisphere, we don't see that sort of natural light until well after the first day of spring, around March 21. But with the aid of grow lights, you can provide enough supplemental indoor light to convince seeds and seedlings that they're out in the sun. The fluorescent bulbs produce a light spectrum similar to that of the sun's rays. Grow lights can be picked up at most local hardware stores and plant shops. Grab the cheap version—a big bulb with a stainless steel shade or backing and a clip. (You can buy the hanging kind if you have the space and time to set up a system to hang it from.) The clip allows you to clasp the grow light onto a dining room chair or other sturdy support and focus the light directly on the seedlings. A timer for your light is also a good investment, unless you're an "early to bed, early to rise" type of person. You may have heard of people using a warming mat under their trays to warm the seed-starting medium, but I don't think this practice is really necessary for the casual gardener, as long as your apartment is warm enough; plus, the grow light will offer some ambient heat.

Seed trays are a must for getting started. They provide the perfect depth for seedlings to grow strong before being transplanted, and you can sow an entire garden's worth of seeds in one go. Using one large seed tray also keeps the process a bit more organized and tidy. Plastic seed trays are made from thin black plastic and have small cells to hold soil and seed. I recommend using just one tray for your first year; it should provide enough space to produce plenty of plants for your garden. Be sure to also purchase the clear plastic cover that fits over each tray. This cover acts as insulation, keeping seeds warm and moist, which is the perfect condition for germination. You will also need the plastic liner for your seedling tray to sit in. This liner will catch and retain any excess water that drains, sparing spillage and helping to keep seedlings moist.

The trays should be filled with a sterile seed-starting mix— which technically is not a soil. These mixes often contain coco coir (coconut-shell fiber), pumice, and perlite. This combination allows for good drainage and air circulation and will readily absorb and retain water. There are no nutrients added to sterile seed mixes—new plants do not need them, as each seed has a small amount of food supply for the plant's early growth.

I set up seed trays on my dining room table in front of my only window—one that faces due east. Any table will do; just be certain you can plug in a grow light nearby. But ambient light from a window is always helpful, so place trays as close to natural light as possible. Rotate the seed tray every few days so plants will not stretch for the light and grow too leggy.

Once you have your seeds, tray, grow light, seed-starting mix, and a dedicated space to grow in, it's time to start planting. Following is a step-by-step guide to starting your own seeds at home.

1. Cover the work surface with newspaper to catch any excess seedling mix. Fill the seed tray about three quarters of the way full with the mix. (You will be adding a bit more mix to cover the sown seeds.) It's easiest to sift seedling mix over the tops of the cells, then run your palm over the top of the cells to

distribute evenly. This will also brush off any excess mix from the divider rims into the cells.

2. Using a small bottle, gently water the entire seed tray, making sure the mix gets thoroughly dampened. It's important to moisten the mix now so it can be weighed down and it has taken up some moisture. If you do this after you've sown your seeds, the water will pool on the surface of the mix, and seeds can easily spill up and over the sides of the plant cells. No big deal, but when a seed gets washed over into the next row, it does make for an interesting game of *what-the-hell-is-this-plant?* after germination.

3. Sow one to two seeds in each cell of the seedling tray, working in rows. I suggest planting only one variety of seed per row, even if you don't fill the row. This will help keep things organized. Each plant cell needs only one or two seeds.

4. Label your seeds as you go. For clever label ideas, check out Chapter 7, Do-It-Yourself Garden.

5. Lightly cover the entire surface with another sprinkle of seed-starting mix, and water very lightly again. As the bottom layer of mix is already moist, the top layer needs only a trickle. You can use a water bottle to spray a fine mist over the top of the seed tray; this gentle method won't disturb the surface or displace any seeds.

6. Cover the tray with the clear plastic top and slightly prop up one corner with a bottle cap or similar item for a bit of ventilation.

7. Set the tray directly under your grow light, and set your grow light to shine for twelve hours. Typically, I time the grow light to run from 6 am to 6 pm, making the most of natural daylight.

8. Keep the top layer of the mix just moist (not wet), never letting it dry out. The clear plastic cover will collect moisture from condensing evaporation. If there is no condensation on the

plastic cover, that is usually a good indicator that you need to mist the tray with more water.

When seedlings are tall enough and hitting the sides of the cover, remove the cover and prepare to harden them off. *Hardening off* means gradually acclimating them to outside conditions. If you moved tender young plants from a warm environment immediately to a cool environment, they would go into shock and falter. Instead, you must adjust them to outside weather conditions slowly. For the first three days of hardening off your seed tray, place it outside, sheltered from wind and rain, during the warmest part of the day for two hours. From the fourth to the sixth day, place your seed tray outside for four hours during the warmest part of the day. On the seventh and eighth days, place them outside for a total of six hours a day. You may have to adapt this depending on weather changes; use common sense. This practice should condition the starts enough to harden them off and prepare them for being planted out in containers.

If the current weather conditions are not conducive to planting out in the garden (i.e., too cold, too wet, etc.), instead of hardening off plants straight away, you can transplant (or *pot up*) the seedlings. Transplant the seedlings into small pots (four-inch pots from the nurseries work great) filled with regular potting soil and keep indoors under a grow light until the weather allows you to harden off the starts and plant them out.

PLANTS TO PROPAGATE FROM CUTTINGS	HERBS TO PROPAGATE BY ROOT DIVISION
Lavender	Chives
Lemon Balm	Lovage
Mint	Marjoram
Scented Geraniums	Oregano
Tarragon	Thyme

Propagation

Propagating a plant from a cutting or root division is one of the coolest parts of gardening. By doing this, you are splitting an existing plant into two or more. When I first tried my hand at propagation, of course I had no idea what I was doing. I clipped a stem off a scented geranium and stuck it inside a small pot filled with potting soil, watered often, and kept my fingers crossed—and it worked! I always feel like I'm getting away with something when I take a small piece from one plant to create a new plant. It's the ultimate garden share.

Propagating plants, quite simply, speaks to a plant's reproduction beyond the usual blooming and seeding. This can be done by splitting the roots of a parent plant (root division) or by taking a cutting. (Grafting is also considered a form of propagation, but you probably won't be starting an apple orchard on your patio anytime soon.) *Vegetative propagation* is an act of asexual reproduction (no seeds required), wherein a leaf, a small piece of root, or a stem will send down roots. To foster this propagation, you must determine if your plant is a good candidate.

SELF-SEEDING ANNUALS

Self-seeding plants are a lazy gardener's dream come true. If you leave plants to flower and drop seed, odds are you'll end up with a brand-new crop of sprouts next spring.

Many edible flowers are self-seeding, which means you need only leave them to reseed to gain many additional plants. When new sprouts grow, you can leave them to flourish, weed them out, or treat them as a hostess gift and repot for others.

Give self-seeding plants a nice big pot, or set an empty container with potting soil directly next to them so the seed has somewhere to drop and germinate come mid- to late summer.

Here are some wonderful, self-seeding edibles:

Borage	Marigold
Chamomile	Nasturtiums
Chervil	Nigella

Many herbs can be divided by splitting their roots. To do this, dig up the plant and its entire root system as best you can in early spring or fall. Growth is slow during these seasons, which makes this treatment easier on the plant. Work apart the roots and slice through them with a clean knife or your hands. Be sure that each division has both healthy roots and at least one small green shoot. Repot into a large enough pot and water well. Be sure to keep it watered well until the plant catches on and begins to put out new growth.

If you already have perennial herb pots going, it may be time for you to split them and separate the cuttings into two pots. Every three years or so perennial herbs do well with some dividing. Add some compost to the new potting mix and repot in the same-size container or larger. If you don't need more of the same herb, divide them anyway and repot some cuttings as gifts for friends or neighbors.

Some plants will root out from their stem, which makes them excellent candidates for cuttings. As a general rule of thumb, take a cutting from new plant growth. This is best done in mid- to late spring or early summer. Cuttings prosper in warm conditions. This also allows enough time for the cutting to put on some new growth without the stress and cold of winter. On some plants new growth comes in the form of a side shoot; in others it grows from the top of the plant's branches. Choose the newest growth and cut about a five-inch length just below a set of leaves. Remove the lowest leaves from the cutting, as well as any buds or blossoms on the stem. (If left, these will take energy away from the plant by producing seed.) Place the cutting directly into a small pot of potting soil (leave it unfertilized for now), being sure to bury the lowest leaf node (the node is the area below the lowest leaves that you just removed) and water well. (The leaf node is where the bulk of the plant's hormones are located, and they will aid in root development.) Keep the cutting watered until the plant begins to put on new growth. When the cutting does not pull out of the soil with a gentle tug, new growth is sufficient for transplanting to a bigger pot; this generally takes from four to six weeks.

Chapter 5

Feeding &
Watering Plants

When I first started gardening at home, I kept flowers that I thought were pretty or exceptionally fragrant. Without much consideration for their care, I put them in random pots I purchased, giving little thought to individual plant needs or my overall success at keeping them alive. As one might suspect, I had plenty of failures and killed plants every year. At some point I decided that I should probably fertilize, so I did what many clueless but well-intentioned home gardeners do—I went to the store and bought a box of Miracle-Gro especially designed for flowers. My dad practically bought stock in Miracle-Gro when we were kids, so I automatically grabbed the product I was familiar with. Interestingly enough, the fertilizer looked like blue crystal. I wasn't sure what was in it, but I knew enough to be very careful not to let any come in contact with my skin. It was like a disco in a box—all bright neon and shiny. When I got home, I tried to follow the directions and add appropriate amounts of fertilizer to water, but really I just guessed and added a few mounded spoonfuls to my watering can. Looking back, it makes me cringe to think about all the chemicals I washed off my deck right into the waters of Lake Union, where I live. I didn't notice any marked difference in my garden that I recall, but it was the first time I considered how best to care for a plant.

Obvious statement number one: Plants are living things. Obvious statement number two: Because plants are living things, they need nourishment to grow and be healthy and productive. Just as we require a bare minimum of calories and hydration in order to survive, plants require certain essentials to put on healthy growth. These include minerals and other nutrients found in healthy soils, sunlight, and water. Without these key components, your plants will suffer.

Containers are not a natural environment in which to grow plants. Your goal as an urban gardener is to mimic their natural soil conditions within the confines of your pots. This entails a fine balance of fertilizer, water, and sun. Each plant has its own particular requirements, as well, so it can be a bit of a brain tease. As with most things, a little education up front will help you grasp how best to care for your plants.

Plants need three main nutrients in order to prosper: nitrogen, phosphorus, and potassium. On fertilizer labels, these are represented by the elemental symbols from the periodic table: NPK. Different plants require varying levels of each. Certain plants are considered "heavy feeders." This refers to their dependence on a particular nutrient. Onions, for instance, are heavy feeders and will do well over time if given a regular supply of nutrients, chiefly nitrogen.

Because containers are continually being flushed (from watering), it's important to keep them on a regular feeding schedule. It is possible, however, to add too much fertilizer to your pots, leading to poor plant health and *burn*, which refers to the shriveled leaves indicative of overfertilization. With any garden, it is best to start out with small amounts of fertilizer and build up if your plants seem listless. In my own apartment garden, I generally add a teaspoon of fertilizer to small pots and a heaping tablespoon to large pots when I first plant or sow something. After that, plan to refertilize about every eight weeks with a gentle organic fertilizer.

Following is a list of necessary nutrients, the role they play in plants, and some suggestions on adding them to your containers.

This is not conclusive, but all suggestions are organic, and easy enough to come by at your local nursery or by using your own resourcefulness.

Nitrogen (N)

As a rule of thumb, leafy green growth is supported by nitrogen. All plants need this, as they all have leafy greens that photosynthesize and convert sunlight to energy that a plant then uses as food. Lettuces need a bit more nitrogen than say, a tomato. We don't eat the green leaves off tomatoes, we eat the fruit; therefore super healthy green leaf support is not our top priority with a tomato plant. Lettuce, on the other hand, is a leafy green that we eat, so it's important to supply a healthy amount of nitrogen. Nitrogen should be added to pots every six to eight weeks. Constant watering will wash away the fertilizer over time. Take a small handful and dust it over the top surface of the soil, then gently work in the fertilizer with a fork.

You can add nitrogen to your apartment garden in a number of ways.

Alfalfa Meal
Alfalfa meal is just that: ground-up alfalfa. These pellets release slowly into the soil over time and have a pretty low level of nitrogen, which is great for containers as it helps to minimize burn. I use alfalfa meal in my pots often because it is considered a gentle fertilizer. This is also a good alternative to fish meal if you're a vegetarian.

Bat Guano
Yeah, it's bat poop. Everyone is obsessed with this form of fertilizer, it seems. I think it's simply a novelty, but in fact it is a decent choice for any garden. This manure is mined from old bat caves and can be expensive. It's a potent fertilizer, however, and has a fair amount of phosphorus, as well, making it a good choice for fruiting plants. Use guano as a top-dressing, to minimize root burn.

Coffee Grounds

Coffee grounds are packed with nitrogen and are a great way to add nutrients to your soil without spending extra money on store-bought fertilizer. One pot of brewed coffee will render enough grounds to sprinkle on top of a large potted plant. Grounds also act as a slug barrier (if you find slugs are an issue in your pots), as slugs don't like to climb over the rough texture. I use the grounds on most of my herbs. Take extra care if using on lettuces, however, because the grounds tend to get in between leaves and can sometimes scent them slightly. Coffee grounds will mix into your soil and break down over time. Coffee grounds also act as mulch (more about mulch shortly), so be careful to keep them away from direct contact with plant stems, which could lead to disease or decay as the grounds break down.

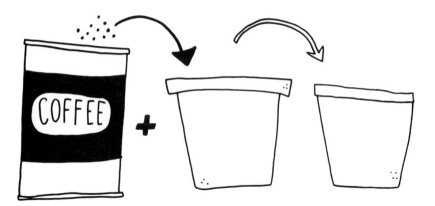

Fish Meal

Fish meal is made from ground-up fish and smells just as you'd think. Fishy! It's a great natural fertilizer made from what would otherwise be waste, and it is said to release slowly in your garden. Great for pots that don't retain nutrients as natural soil will, fish meal is widely available and inexpensive. Most small nurseries carry it in bulk, so you can purchase it in small amounts as needed.

Grass Clippings

Green leafy plants contain nitrogen, remember? So grass clippings are an excellent source of natural nitrogen. Grab your lawn-mowing neighbor (preferably one who uses natural lawn care and doesn't spray pesticides) and arrange to pick up a yard-waste bagful in the spring. It should last you at least through midsummer. Grass clippings can be placed directly on the surface of the pot's soil and left to break down. This decaying process has the added benefit of introducing microorganisms to your pots, which is good for your plants. For real. As with coffee grounds, be mindful to keep clippings away from direct contact with plant stems, where they can lead to disease or decay as they break down.

Phosphorous (P)

Phosphorous promotes the healthy fruiting and flowering of plants. It does this by converting carbohydrates in plants to sugars. If you think about it, snap peas, zucchini, and so on are all fruiting plants whose vegetables have a sweet taste. It's this conversion, helped by direct sun exposure, that is instigated by the presence of phosphorous.

Bone Meal

Bone meal is made from bone and has been used for years as a fertilizer in gardens. A by-product from the slaughterhouse, although bone meal may sound unappetizing, it is actually a great way to use something that would otherwise be wasted. Bones have a high calcium content, as well, and also offer some nitrogen to the soil.

Fish Bone Meal

This mixture is the same as bone meal, but made from the bones of fish.

Rock Phosphate

Vegetarians may balk at using meat and fish industry by-products, so I offer rock phosphate as a vegetarian solution for the vegetable garden. Rock phosphate is generally available in larger quantities, so it's admittedly cumbersome to store for the small apartment garden. Additionally, it is best used in proper soil (meaning, not in pots) because soil will hold onto this nutrient and slowly release it for years. In pots, this is not a perfect solution, as you will flush the soil from repeated watering and will likely add new soil to your pots each year. Still, it is not a bad option, should the other materials not appeal to you.

Potassium (K)

Potassium encourages strong plant growth and a sturdy plant in general. When plants lack potassium, photosynthesis slows down and may weaken their stems. In fact, a weak plant stem is often an early sign of a potassium deficiency. I use potassium in all of my pots—a heaping tablespoon for the large pots and a teaspoon for the mid-sized to smaller pots. If I notice weak plant stems, I'll add a spoonful or two, as it's difficult to overfertilize with potassium. Here are two easy-to-find resources.

Granite Dust

Just as the name implies, this dust is collected at quarries as a by-product. Granite will help build reserves of potassium in your plants, but it's a long, slow process, so it makes sense to use only in your largest pots. Considering that, I much prefer kelp meal.

Kelp Meal

Harvested from the sea, kelp meal is dried and ground up seaweed. It is complete with an abundance of trace minerals, which is also good for the garden. (Remember, plants take up nutrients through their roots, so in theory any nutrients you add to the soil will be taken up by the root and eventually ingested by *you!*) Not only will kelp meal add these micronutrients to your food, but it also supplies a small amount of potassium to your plants. Even better, kelp meal is widely available and can often be found in bulk.

Microorganisms—The Good Bacteria

It is also important to try to introduce microorganisms to your pots when you can. Microorganisms—composed of bacteria and fungi, among others, have several different functions in the garden. They aerate soil, break down organic matter so it is easily digestible to plants, and support healthy root systems. Containers do not naturally invite decomposers and microorganisms to them, as the purchased potting medium is not part of a functioning ecosystem. When is the last time you saw an earthworm in a pot? Although it's a challenge to get these tiny helpers into your container garden, you can increase your odds by creating an environment that will attract them.

Microorganisms are attracted to the process of decomposition of organic matter. In fact, they aid in that process, and the results will ultimately feed your plants. To manufacture a hospitable environment, you need only introduce a steady supply of organic matter and, even better, decaying or decayed organic matter. You can do this by adding 'greens' or other organic matter to your pots. Greens come in the form of chopped weeds and, as mentioned earlier, lawn clippings and spent coffee grounds. Sprinkle a handful over the top of the soil around the base of your plants (carefully leaving the area right around the plant stems bare). Over time, without any maintenance, these added greens will start to break down and decompose. Eventually you can fork this decomposed matter into your potting soil and continue adding more on top. It is good to note that microorganism activity increases with the ambient temperature. The work they do grinds to a halt in winter, as both plants and organisms fall dormant, and begins to pick up again in spring. Activity will continue to increase as temperatures rise into the summer, so be sure to gather greens to keep on hand for adding to your pots during the warmer months. I typically fill a large yard-waste bag full of grass clippings in spring (from a friend's yard) and keep it handy on my deck.

Green Manure

Green manure is a term used for a fast-growing cover crop (a crop that is used to cover bare earth) that is eventually turned into the soil to decay, like compost. In this fashion, microorganisms and nutrients are added to the soil. For a container gardener, this concept is a bit much to put into practice; it's easier to sprinkle a handful of compost or coffee grounds in your containers. But green manure does more than add nutrients. Growing a complimentary green at the base of other crops suppresses weeds (and yes, weeds *will* find their way into your containers!), helps to hold in water, and contributes to aerating the soil. These crops also aid in the regulation of soil temperature, keeping it warmer in winter and cooler in summer. Green manure is also beneficial if you choose a flowering variety like buckwheat. For larger plants like cucumbers, I often distribute a few pinches of buckwheat seed along the perimeter of the container. If your container has a smaller plant, like lettuce, try Huia white clover, which grows densely and won't grow tall enough to block sun from the lettuce plants.

Winter Mulching

In winter, I switch over to a brown mulch—a more durable organic material that will hold up and insulate my plants in the cooler months. Winter mulches prevent nutrients from being leached out of the pot and help minimize compaction from winter snow and rain. In an in-ground garden plot, winter mulches are very important. For a container garden, winter mulches act more as insulation to protect perennial plant roots from freezing temperatures.

Fallen leaves are readily available and easy to come by, and you can spread them across the entire container surface to protect the potting soil. They will likely not decompose over winter, so come spring be sure to remove them from the containers and put them in your regular compost. Cardboard and newspaper also work well; you can shred or tear them and lay them directly on the soil surface. Be sure to use only the black-and-white print, as colored ink can be harmful. Shredded paper will break down rather quickly, so you can leave any residual paper come spring and it will soon decay, at which point you can dig it into the soil like compost.

Home Composting

Compost, as any gardener will tell you, is one of the single most important additions to a healthy, sustainable garden. It is the great equalizer, taking in the bad and processing it into something good.

What follows may be a bit overwhelming for the casual gardener, but as you dig in you will learn that compost is truly fascinating. This lush brown medium acts as fertilizer, insulates plants, suppresses weeds, and retains moisture. Although a small-scale urban gardener growing plants in pots doesn't necessarily have to devote a lot of thought to compost, it's nice to understand just what it is and how it can work for you so you can make educated choices about when to use it and why.

Compost is essentially made up of organic matter (from plants and animals) that has been broken down over time. There are many players in this process—animals, fungi, bugs, microbes, bacteria—all of whom play a part in the decomposition of organic matter that results in compost.

There are two basic methods for making compost: hot and cold. A hot compost pile produces *finished* compost (ready for garden use) more quickly. The hot composting method generates internal heat, which accelerates the process of breaking down the organic matter. Using the right mixture of carbon and nitrogen (that is, browns like dried leaves and greens like lawn clippings), hot compost heats up by feeding off carbon. When it eventually burns out, nitrogen-rich compounds are left behind. Now, if you've been reading straight through from the beginning, you know that leafy greens need nitrogen to grow strong, productive plants. So this hot-processed compost is a very beneficial addition to any garden.

Cold compost is created in the same way as hot compost, but at a much slower rate, as it is a passive process. Cold compost does not "burn" carbon, but instead relies on the slow work of decomposers to break down organic matter and convert it into compost over time.

Of the two processes, cold compost is certainly the easiest. You simply dig a hole in the ground and add vegetable food waste and green and brown yard waste, then cover it up.

In a small garden, however—particularly one with no actual garden soil—none of these processes are really possible. But that doesn't necessarily exclude an urban gardener from the compost game. *Vermiculture* is another great resource for making compost at home in a very small space. Vermiculture uses worms in a worm bin to break down food waste and bedding into compost. Worms produce castings: worm manure, also called *vermicompost*. These castings are then collected and used on plants and in gardens as lush, nitrogen-dense fertilizer.

A worm bin has the added benefit of being small; it can be stored inside or outside. So it's an excellent option for apartment and condo dwellers who want to compost at home.

Worms can eat half their weight in food waste every day. If you start off with one pound of worms, count on their handling about a half a pound of kitchen scraps each day. There are a number of options for worm bins, from pricey commercial bins with multiple trays to plastic storage bins or homemade bins. (For instructions on building a worm bin and filling it with proper bedding, see Chapter 7, Do-It-Yourself Garden.) All systems need some method of drainage, because worms generate liquid waste, and if conditions get too mucky, the worms will not be happy. The worms used in worm bins are not your garden earthworms, but a particular species—commonly called red worms or red wigglers—that would not survive for long in outdoor conditions. You can buy them locally or by mail order, but the cheapest (free!) source is from a gardener who already has a worm bin going.

It is important to note that a new worm bin starts off slowly, so you should add food waste in small amounts at first and monitor how quickly the worms are able to process them. They may ignore foods they don't like; if so, remove these scraps from the bin so they don't rot and give off odors. When you add food to the bin, lift some bedding and put food scraps underneath. This will help minimize odors. Additionally, when adding scraps you should utilize a different part of the bin than the last time, so the worms have a chance to process the older scraps before more waste is piled over them. Plan to follow a pattern, moving from left to right and then right to left, back and forth through the bin.

Worms can get finicky about what they will or won't eat. A few finely crushed eggshells provide grit to help them digest, as worms do not have teeth. Do not give the worms proteins, dairy, oil, or oily products like vegetables cooked in oil or fried potato chips. Instead, include only plant-based organic matter like vegetable and fruit scraps. I have seen many a worm ignore citrus peels, but you can try them. Worms also love coffee grounds, and you can include the paper filters. Grains (stale bread, tortillas, and so on) are OK too.

Keep your worms in a temperate location, ranging from 55°F to 75°F; this means you may need to bring an outdoor bin inside during cold winter months.

After a few months, the worm compost will likely appear dark brown, like finely crushed cookie crumbs. This can take up to six months. To harvest your compost and re-bed the bin, move the entire contents of the bin over to one side. On the other side, refill the area with a mound of fresh bedding. Add some new kitchen waste to the new bedding side and wait for the worms to migrate over. This can take anywhere from two weeks to the better part of a month. Worm compost can be used on all potted plants and even indoor plants.

Top-dress your pots with a sprinkling of worm compost every six weeks or so. As worm castings are quite nutrient rich, you want to be sure not to add too much too often or you run the risk of plant burn from overfertilization.

As mentioned earlier, worms also expel liquid as they work to break down your kitchen scraps. You can collect that liquid and add it directly to plants along with the vermicompost. Or add equal parts water to the worm "tea" and spray or water your plants with this solution. This also makes a great gift for any gardeners in your life.

Watering Schedule

Water, it is quite obvious, is crucial to healthy plant growth and a successful garden. Water transports minerals to a plant, allows evaporation for cooling, and aids in photosynthesis. Water's function to any plant is of utmost importance. With the confinement of containers, plants will need extra attention, as water drains out quickly and pots allow individual plants more exposure to sun, wind, and heat than a traditional garden environment. Water may also evaporate from pots, which is why container material (see page 9) also plays a role in determining the water needs for each plant. With that, there are some basic principles to follow when watering your containers.

Rule #1: Water Regularly

It is imperative that potting soil not go completely dry at any point in a plant's life cycle. Allowing your potting soil to get bone dry increases the odds of soil compaction, thereby reducing the odds of water retention. With a compacted potted plant, water will often collect on the surface and pool down the sides of a container instead of moistening the soil uniformly. Any medium with peat is particularly susceptible to compaction. To avoid drying out your pots, be sure to check for water daily by inserting a finger into the pot. Soil should feel damp (not overly wet) about two inches down. If the soil is dry, water.

Rule #2: Water Deeply

Add enough water to your pots that some water seeps out of the drainage holes. This ensures a full watering so that roots in the bottom of the container can take up water. If you only water to a shallow depth, you increase the odds that your plant will have shallow roots. Shallow roots lead to weakened plants. And weakened plants have a diminished harvest. It's a bad cycle to start and it is challenging to eradicate. It is better to water fully and deeply every two to three days than to give your plants a little sprinkle every day.

Rule #3: Do Not Overwater

Overwatering plants waterlogs the soil and prohibits oxygen from flowing freely to the roots of plants. Plants need oxygen to survive, so this is a bad problem. In a short matter of time, waterlogging leads to decay and rot. Not good. To ensure that you do not overwater your plants, check for dryness in the soil before you water. Also, make sure you have proper drainage and that water is flowing through your container. You can also check the bottom of your pots for excess moisture. Turn the pots over every now and again and feel through the drainage holes for dampness. If the soil is too wet, give it a day or two to be absorbed by the plant and evaporated before watering again.

Rule #4: Timing is Everything

Plants' water needs will change with the seasons and depend on sun exposure and the size and material of your container, so there is no steadfast rule on how often you should be watering. You must be your own best decision maker to craft the best watering schedule. However, seasons will often dictate a commonsense approach. Plants need more water in summer (when it is hot and soil dries out faster) than in fall (when the days are shorter and less warm). In fact, plants may need two daily waterings in summer, depending on your sun exposure. Rooftop containers will get much warmer than an east-facing balcony. Use your better judgment. As a general rule, however, plants will do much better if you water first thing in the morning before it gets too warm. This allows for a proper soaking and eliminates immediate evaporation due to heat. It also allows time for water to work its way through the pot so that you are not causing 'wet feet' or overly damp roots to sit overnight and cool. In some regions, cold nights will cool wet soil and cause stress to heat-lovers like beans, zucchini, and cucumbers. Conversely, leafy greens often appreciate an early-evening cool down (and will show signs of water and heat stress by wilting and shriveling along the leaf's edge). For the ultimate rule of thumb, plan to water every morning, and only water in the evening if a plant is really suffering from heat, which can happen in the height of summer.

Rule #5: Find a Friend to Help

If you leave town in summer, you must find someone to water your plants. You can set up your own self-watering system at home for short weekend jaunts (see Water Bottle Redux project, page 157), but if you're taking a holiday in the high season of summer, make sure to have a friend or neighbor come over and water. It is quite possible that plants will die in a matter of days if not properly watered when it's consistently hot out, so do yourself a favor and have someone tend the garden for you. You can always trade them some homegrown goodies for their efforts.

Chapter 6

Recipes from the Garden

Keeping a patio garden is a labor of love. Containers need more attention than a garden plot does. Sun exposure is often limited, watering must be monitored almost daily, and efficient use of limited space can be a challenge. Speaking for myself, there is a lot of tripping over pots and materials on my deck! In the end, however, it is worth it. I experience sweet satisfaction every time I harvest something from my garden and make a meal. It is refreshing to not have to run to the store for something green. It's also very nice to be influenced by what's available. I don't always know what to make for a meal, but with a quick glance out to the garden, I often find an answer or, at the very least, inspiration.

Plants do better when you actively harvest from them or prune them back. Most plants continue putting on growth and bearing fruit when harvested regularly. This is a good thing, as it means kitchens are in constant supply in the high season of summer.

Once you have your own garden going, you'll learn that plants will dictate what you're eating, not the other way around. Lettuce is ready when it's ready, so now you get to enjoy a salad. Borage leaves are young and tender only for a few weeks, so during that time you had best figure out how to incorporate them into your meals. If you let these windows of opportunity pass you by, you run the risk of bolted, bitter, or poorly flavored food.

When thinking about garden recipes, I follow a few basic principles. I like to keep it fresh and let flavors shine through. For me, the simpler the recipe, the better. My guess is that most people don't like overly complicated food, and when you're cooking with herbs and flowers you needn't do much to highlight their flavor. I also like to use as much of the plant as possible. Stems, leaves, flowers, all of it. If I let something go too long and its leaves are yellowed, I use that, too. Make it your goal to leverage all the energy you've put into keeping the plant alive and well; you can do this by using every last bit to your advantage.

Admittedly, some of the plants in Chapter 3, What to Grow, For Real, are not familiar choices for most people. I've included a lot of flowers and herbs because those plants do well in containers. They may well be completely new to you, and so we get to the adventure of experimentation in the garden and the kitchen. This is a great opportunity to expand horizons and try something new. Eat something different. Challenge your palate in a new way. Make sure to pick leaves off your plants as they grow to see what they taste like. Only you know what you like!

I have included recipes that are both simple and delicious. The recipes are seasonal, as well, drawing on crops that will be ready at the same time. Zucchini comes in right about the time that borage is vigorous, so I came up with a simple tart recipe using both that you can make for an appetizer, lunch, or a light dinner. In a perfect world, all ingredients should work together as a seasonal dish. Each recipe is followed by some suggestions for incorporating your harvest into other meals. Try them all.

Zucchini Fritters

This is an easy recipe to use up a garden glut of zucchini (a wonderful container plant) and odds and ends of herbs you have growing. It's also light and summery. Feel free to experiment with the herbs you use, but go for a mix of tender herbs (such as mint or tarragon) rather than those that prefer some cooking time (like the hardier sage and thyme). The recipe multiplies easily, so you can also adjust the quantity of this dish up given the number of guests you're feeding.

Makes 4 to 6 fritters

> 3 tablespoons olive oil, plus more for frying
>
> ½ onion, finely chopped (about 1 cup)
>
> Salt
>
> 2 cups finely diced zucchini (about 2 medium)
>
> 2 eggs
>
> 2 tablespoons flour, all-purpose or whole wheat
>
> ¼ teaspoon freshly ground black pepper
>
> ¼ cup chopped fresh herb mix—mint, anise hyssop, tarragon

Place a large sauté pan over medium heat, and add the olive oil. Add the onions and a pinch of salt. Sauté until the onions are soft and translucent, 8 to 10 minutes. Add the zucchini and another pinch of salt. Sauté until the zucchini is soft and nearly cooked through, another 3 minutes. Remove from the heat and spread in a single layer on a sheet pan to cool to room temperature.

In a medium bowl, whisk together the eggs, flour, pepper, and herbs. Fold the cooled zucchini mixture into the eggs until all has been incorporated. You should have a thin batter that holds together but is loose.

Heat a large skillet over medium heat and cover the bottom with a thin layer of olive oil. When the pan is hot, add small ladles full of zucchini batter to form fritters about 4 inches in diameter. Fry on both sides, about 4 to 5 minutes per side, until golden brown. Repeat with the remaining batter. Serve immediately.

More Garden Recipes: Zucchini tastes great raw and is wonderful in summertime salads. For a quick *panzanella* salad (bread salad), cut zucchini into small cubes and toss with some crushed tomatoes, croutons, mint, and basil, and dress simply with olive oil and red wine vinegar.

Chive Butter and Radish Toasts

This appetizer is a simple way to pull together a little nosh for guests if in a pinch for time. Chives and radishes are among the first vegetables available in spring.

Makes 24 toasts

> 2 tablespoons finely chopped chives
> 4 tablespoons unsalted butter, at room temperature
> Baguette, cut into thin slices
> 1 bunch radishes, trimmed of greens and washed well
> Coarse sea salt

Preheat the oven to 400°F. Combine the chives and butter in a small bowl and mash together with the back of a spoon until well blended. Refrigerate to firm up.

Lay the baguette slices in a single layer on a large sheet pan and bake until crispy and just beginning to brown at the edges, about 12 minutes. Remove and let cool completely. While the crostini are cooling, slice the radishes using the thinnest setting of a mandoline. If you don't have a mandoline, slice them with a knife as thin as possible, so they're almost see-through. When the crostini are completely cooled, smear the tops with a thin layer of chive butter. Lay the radish slices on top, overlapping the layers slightly. Sprinkle with sea salt and set on a platter.

Continue layering crostini, chive butter, radishes, and salt until you run out of radishes. Serve immediately. Store any leftover chive butter, wrapped tightly in plastic wrap, in your freezer.

More Garden Recipes: Chives are the ultimate garnish for many dishes. They pair exceptionally well with red meat—think grilled steak or even a burger—as they have a strong onion flavor. Chives are also excellent over simple boiled potatoes. Forgo the butter and stir fork-mashed boiled potatoes with chives and salt.

Salt and Nigella Flatbread

This quick recipe can be whipped together in a hurry. These flatbreads are reminiscent of pita bread, but not nearly as doughy. They are made with whole wheat flour, which makes them dense and hardy. Nigella seeds have a slight onion taste and are beautiful seeds to use as garnish for this flatbread.

Makes 10 to 12 flatbreads

> 1½ cups whole wheat flour
>
> ½ cup all-purpose flour
>
> 1 tablespoon olive oil, plus more for brushing (or melted butter)
>
> Scant ¾ cup warm water
>
> Coarse sea salt
>
> 2 tablespoons nigella seeds

Combine the flours, olive oil, and water in the bowl of an electric mixer fitted with a dough hook and knead on medium-slow setting for 5 to 7 minutes, until all the flour is incorporated and the dough is elastic, not wet. Remove from the bowl, cover with a cloth, and set aside to rest for one hour.

Preheat the oven to 400°F. Set a sheet pan in the oven to heat. Cut off pieces of dough into small balls—about the size of a Ping-Pong ball. On a lightly floured surface, roll each ball into a thin flat disk, about 5 inches across. When you have five or six disks of dough, remove the sheet pan from the oven and place the disks on the hot pan. Bake until the edges are just golden brown, 8 to 10 minutes. Continue baking the rest of the dough in this fashion.

While the flatbreads are still warm, brush one side with olive oil, sprinkle with salt, and finish with a sprinkling of nigella seeds. Serve warm or hold at room temperature.

More Garden Recipes: Nigella seeds make wonderful garnishes for soups or savory vegetable dishes. Crushed into a paste, they also pair nicely with cooked-down plums as a side dish for a cheese plate.

Pea Vine Dumplings

Many cultures include savory cakes and dumplings in their cuisine. My family in Croatia eats burek—*a strudel-like dough stuffed with a savory filling like meat and onion, or something sweet like apples. When I was little, my Aunt Janet used to fry us up some* frites *filled with ham and mozzarella, just as she learned from her Italian mother-in-law. Really, any dough stuffed with something and fried is guaranteed to be the bomb.*

Pea plants are easy to grow in containers, and while you grow them for the peas, you can also clip tender vines from the plant to sauté. This recipe takes that one step further and makes use of older pea vines that are strong and slightly woody. Normally we would never eat them, but broken down and cooked in this recipe, they shine. These fried dumplings are a great way to use the entire plant. You can use other hardy greens for this recipe—wild dandelion greens would work. (If they are very bitter, temper their bite with a sweet vinegar like sherry or some honey before adding to the dumplings.) This is a dumpling dough, not a yeasted dough, so it will not be soft and flaky. Be sure to let the dough rest for at least an hour before shaping and frying. If you don't want to be stuck waiting while the dough rests, make it the night before, cover it with plastic wrap, and leave it on the counter overnight.

Makes 12 dumplings

Dough

½ cup all-purpose flour

½ cup whole wheat pastry flour

Pinch salt

¼ to ½ cup warm water

Filling

2 tablespoons olive oil

½ onion, finely chopped (about 1 cup)

½ pound pea vines, coarsely chopped (about 4 cups)

Scant ½ cup water

¼ teaspoon ground cumin

¼ teaspoon ground coriander

¼ teaspoon smoked paprika

Salt and freshly ground black pepper

Vegetable oil for frying

Mix the flours and salt in large bowl or pulse in the bowl of an electric mixer. Add the water in increments and work by hand until the dough comes together or, with the mixer running, add a little bit of water at a time until the dough comes together in one ball. Once you have a ball of dough, knead on a floured work surface until the dough is elastic and smooth, about 10 minutes. Cover with plastic wrap or a damp towel and let sit on the counter for at least an hour, up to overnight.

To make the filling, cover the bottom of a large sauté pan with the olive oil and set over medium-high heat. Add half of the onions and all of the pea vines and cook, stirring often, so the pea vines and onions do not stick. Once the pea vines are fairly broken down and the onions are beginning to soften, add the water and turn the heat up to high. Bring to a boil, then reduce heat to a simmer and cover the pan. (Because the pea vines are thick and woody, you are cooking them down to soften them.)

Cook covered, until the pea vines are soft and the water is nearly evaporated, 15 to 20 minutes. Remove the lid and turn up the heat to dry out the greens and onions and steam off any extra water. Stir often. When the pan is dry and the greens are beginning to stick, transfer the mixture to a large bowl. Add the remaining onions, cumin, coriander, and paprika. Season to taste with salt and pepper and let cool.

To make the dumplings, cut the dough into twelve small pieces and roll into balls between your palms. Lightly flour your hands if the dough sticks. On a lightly floured work surface, roll out balls of dough into small rounds 4 or 5 inches in diameter.

Working with one round at a time, place a spoonful of pea vine filling in the center. Fold the dough in half. Working from the middle out, press the sides together to create a seal. (By doing this, you are pushing out any air to prevent the dumplings from breaking open while they're frying.) You can pinch the edges with your fingers or use the back of a fork to press a design in the dough and make sure the seal holds.

Over medium-high heat, heat about 1 inch of vegetable oil in a deep-sided sauté pan. When the oil is hot, but not smoking, slip in about four dumplings—as many as will fit without overcrowding—and fry until golden brown, 4 to 5 minutes. Flip over with a slotted spoon and fry the other side until golden brown, about another 5 minutes. Lift out with a slotted spoon and drain on a paper bag. Fry the remaining dumplings and serve hot or at room temperature.

The dumplings can be made several hours ahead and fried when ready, or frozen, wrapped tightly in a plastic bag, to fry at a later date.

More Garden Recipes: Older pea vines can also be cooked as above and used as a side dish. Omit spices and instead add a handful of toasted pine nuts and a squeeze of lemon.

Sides

Warm Peas and Lemon Balm

Shelling peas are one of those vegetables that are just perfect when homegrown. Frozen peas do not compare to fresh peas that are sweet and crispy, even when cooked briefly in a water bath as called for here. It is a bit of a labor-intensive process to first blanch, then shock the peas in an ice-water bath, but it's worth it for the crisp-tender texture this extra step produces. Peas also pair beautifully with mint. You can easily substitute mint for the lemon balm in this recipe, or use equal amounts of both herbs.

Serves 2 to 4

> 1 pound shelling peas
> 1 tablespoon butter
> 1 tablespoon finely chopped lemon balm leaves
> Salt and freshly ground black pepper

Bring a pot of salted water to a boil. While the water is boiling, shell the peas. Set up a water bath, filling a large bowl with cold water and ice. Set aside. When the peas have been hulled, drop them into the boiling water and cook until bright green and floating, 2 to 3 minutes. Drain and immediately drop them into the ice-water bath, halting the cooking process. Give them a stir to make sure they are cool, then drain and set aside.

In a medium skillet over medium heat, melt the butter. Add the lemon balm and stir until the leaves make a popping sound, 2 to 3 minutes. Add the peas and stir to combine. When the peas are just heated through, about 1 minute, remove from heat and season to taste with salt and pepper. Serve immediately.

More Garden Recipes: Lemon balm is a strong herb, so it's best to use it sparingly. For a summer sun tea, combine torn mint and lemon balm leaves, add water, and steep in the sun.

Carrots with Honey and Chervil

I like to use small carrots in this recipe, and spring is a great time to get some. Farmers have thinned carrots from the field, and often you can pick up these immature carrots at the farmers' markets for cheap. Aim to purchase the smallest carrots of the bunch. If you can't find baby carrots, quarter large carrots so you end up with evenly sized carrot sticks. This recipe takes advantage of blanching the carrots, so the final texture is crisp-tender—not quite cooked, but not quite raw. Warming up butter and honey gives them a touch of sweetness that works well with the flavor of the chervil. You can substitute parsley for chervil if you miss the season—chervil is available in early spring and sometimes in July after it reseeds itself.

Serves 4 to 6

1 pound small carrots, peeled
1 tablespoon butter
1 teaspoon honey
1 tablespoon roughly chopped fresh chervil
Salt and freshly ground black pepper

Set up an ice-water bath—combine cold water and a handful of ice in a large bowl.

Bring a pot of salted water to boil. Add the carrots and blanch until just tender, about 4 minutes. Strain and immediately plunge the carrots into the ice-water bath. Stir occasionally until cool. Drain and set aside.

In a medium sauté pan, melt the butter over medium-high heat. Stir in the honey. Add the carrots and cook until just warmed through, stirring continuously. Remove from the heat and stir in the chervil. Season to taste with salt and pepper. Serve immediately.

More Garden Recipes: Chervil is a great match for eggs—scrambled, hard-boiled, you name it. Chervil also makes a lovely garnish for simple broth soups. For an easy and light meal, heat up some chicken stock until hot, pour in a whisked egg, and cook until the egg forms ribbons in the soup, about 2 minutes. Garnish with chervil.

Crispy Marjoram Potatoes

This is one of my favorite ways to cook potatoes. The trick is to put the potatoes cut side down in a sauté pan over medium heat (not hotter or they'll burn!) and leave them be. No touching! The potatoes end up golden brown and crispy but remain fluffy and sweet inside like a mashed potato. Potatoes and marjoram are a great match. For this recipe, I cook half the marjoram with the potatoes and add half to the finished dish for extra herby flavor. You can double up this batch to serve a crowd, but make sure you keep the potatoes in a single layer in the pan. You may need to use two pans to accommodate them all.

Serves 4

> 2 tablespoons olive oil
> 1 tablespoon butter
> 1 pound Yukon Gold or fingerling potatoes, sliced in half lengthwise
> Salt and freshly ground black pepper
> 2 tablespoons chopped fresh marjoram, divided

Preheat the oven to 350°F. In a large ovenproof sauté pan over medium heat, heat the olive oil and butter. When the butter is melted and hot, place potatoes into the pan in a single layer, cut side down. Sprinkle with some salt and cook until a sharp knife almost pierces the center, 8 to 10 minutes. The potatoes will still give resistance and be raw in the middle. Sprinkle 1 tablespoon of the marjoram over the potatoes and place the entire pan in the oven.

Bake until a sharp knife easily pierces through the flesh, 10 to 15 minutes. Remove from the oven and transfer to a shallow serving bowl. Toss in the remaining marjoram and stir to combine. Season to taste with salt and pepper and serve.

More Garden Recipes: Marjoram is a natural herb for any Italian dish. For a quick tomato sauce, sauté garlic in olive oil, add a can or jar of stewed tomatoes, and finish it with a few tablespoons of marjoram. Marjoram also tastes great with chicken; try substituting marjoram in the Thyme-Roasted Chicken Legs with Charred Onions recipe (page 100).

Smoky Chickpeas with Greens

Miner's lettuce is a succulent green that grows wild but can be cultivated in a garden. It is one of the first greens to pop up in late winter or early spring, so it is perfect for a garden salad after months of no fresh greens. Miner's lettuce has smooth, lily-pad-like leaves and firm crisp stems. Their greens will hold their shape, even after the addition of an acid, making them an excellent addition to legume salads. In this recipe, the acid from a lemon cuts the bite from the raw onion. The addition of chickpeas makes for a light lunch. This is an easy recipe to multiply for guests.

Serves 1

3 thin slices red onion
½ lemon, zested and juiced

3 tablespoons olive oil

¼ teaspoon smoked paprika

¼ teaspoon salt

½ cup chickpeas, cooked

1 cup miner's lettuce or other spring lettuces

Salt and freshly ground black pepper

In large bowl, combine the onion and lemon juice. Let stand for 5 to 10 minutes. Then add the lemon zest, olive oil, paprika, salt, and chickpeas. Stir well and let sit for at least 15 minutes. Toss in the miner's lettuce and stir to blend. Season to taste with salt and pepper and serve immediately.

More Garden Recipes: Miner's lettuce goes nicely with other early and hardy greens like arugula. Make a simple salad using both greens and whatever herbs you have around. Miner's lettuce is also a decent substitute for watercress in recipes. Try adding some leaves to a creamy potato soup and blending.

Pickled Cucumber and Toasted Sesame Salad

I make this salad all the time, and my friends are always calling me for the "recipe." Typically, they're shocked to find out how few ingredients there are. "That's it?" they all ask in disbelief. Essentially what you're doing is quickly pickling the cucumbers in rice wine vinegar. The added touch of toasty flavor comes from both sesame oil and toasted sesame seeds. You could easily forgo the seeds if you don't have them handy.

Serves 2 to 4

3 tablespoons rice wine vinegar

2 teaspoons sugar

1 pound cucumbers, peeled and sliced thin

1 teaspoon sesame oil

1 teaspoon sesame seeds, toasted

In a shallow bowl, combine the vinegar and sugar. Add the cucumbers and toss to coat. Set aside to macerate for 30 minutes or so, stirring often to rotate the cucumber slices. After 30 minutes, add the sesame oil and toasted sesame seeds. Stir to combine and serve.

More Garden Recipes: Cucumbers can be finely diced and combined with tarragon for a relish on grilled fish in the summer. Or chop cucumbers finely and stir with some plain yogurt for a dipping sauce for zucchini fritters. In a fresh salad or raw soup, cucumbers also pair nicely with melons.

Minted Arugula Salad

Arugula and mint work beautifully together. One leaf is spicy, the other cooling. This salad can be chopped fine and used as a garnish on sliced tomatoes or grilled meat. The two can be blended into a pesto for marinating fish or tossing with pasta. (Both of those variations will require a bit more olive oil than indicated here.) Another option is to leave the greens whole, as I've done here for a side salad. Feel free to play with proportions. Salads are meant to be easy affairs. I seldom measure ingredients; I just figure one handful of greens per person.

Serves 2 as a small salad

> 1 cup arugula
> ¼ cup mint leaves, torn
> 2 tablespoons olive oil
> ½ lemon, zested and juiced
> Salt and freshly ground black pepper

Place the arugula, mint, olive oil, lemon juice, and lemon zest in a large mixing bowl and toss to blend. Season to taste with salt and pepper. Serve immediately.

More Garden Recipes: Arugula is a great green to add flavor and texture to your salads. If your plant goes to flower, pick off small leaves and use the white flower heads in salads. Because its flavor is so strong, you can also incorporate arugula into soups. Make a white bean soup and add a handful or two of arugula when you blend it smooth. It adds a nice spicy note.

--- --- --- --- --- --- --- --- --- --- --- --- --- --- --- --- ---

Roasted Shiitakes with Fennel Blossoms

Roasted mushrooms are an easy and flavorful side dish any time of the year. Shiitakes are widely cultivated and available all year long. They don't have much moisture, so they bake up to a chewy-crisp texture quickly. For this recipe, mushrooms are roasted until the stems just begin to brown. Fennel blossoms can be collected in summer and kept as a spice in the pantry. They impart a sweet fennel flavor and aroma to these mushrooms that is quite distinct, as well as phenomenally flavorful.

Serves 4

> 2 pounds shiitake mushrooms, roughly torn into pieces
> 1 teaspoon salt
> ½ teaspoon freshly ground black pepper
> 1 tablespoon fennel blossoms
> 3 tablespoons olive oil

Preheat the oven to 400°F. Toss the mushrooms, salt, pepper, fennel blossoms, and oil in a large bowl, coating the mushrooms evenly. Spread out on a sheet pan, in a single layer, and bake for 30 to 40 minutes, tossing occasionally, until the mushrooms are shriveled and their stems are starting to crisp. They will have released most of their moisture and shrunk in size. Serve immediately or hold at room temperature until serving.

More Garden Recipes: Fennel blossoms are a great herb to add to pork or a white fish like halibut. A light sprinkle of blossoms will also add a complementary flavor to vegetable soups.

Herby Pasta with Lettuce and Prosciutto

This recipe was one of those happy accidents I made one day. I didn't have much in the pantry, and I started just throwing ingredients into a pan. I left onions and prosciutto to sit and get crispy, then doused them with some pasta water to make a thick broth. At the last minute, I added handfuls of lettuce to the pot—a great way to incorporate greens into a pasta dish. Use whatever greens you have on hand—Bibb lettuce, romaine, radicchio, arugula, parsley, mint, basil, lovage, and so on. This is also a great way to use up any lettuce that may be starting to bolt and turn bitter or has begun to wilt with age. Choose a shaped pasta (bowtie is my favorite), not a long noodle.

Serves 4

    3 tablespoons olive oil

    1 tablespoon butter

    5 garlic cloves, peeled and sliced

    1 shallot

    4 slices prosciutto, torn into pieces

    1 tablespoon dry vermouth

    4 cups bowtie or other shaped pasta

    4 cups mixed lettuce greens

    ½ cup mixed herbs

    Parmesan for garnish (optional)

Boil a pot of salted water for the pasta.

In large sauté pan with high sides, heat the olive oil and butter over medium-high heat. When the butter is melted and starting to bubble, add the garlic and shallot. Sauté until cooked and starting to brown at the edges, about 8 to 10 minutes. Add the prosciutto and let sit, stirring only occasionally, allowing it to get brown and crispy, about 4 minutes. When the mixture starts to stick to the bottom of the pan, deglaze with the vermouth and scrape up any brown bits. Cook the vermouth down for 1 minute, then remove the pan from the heat.

Drop the pasta into the boiling water and cook until just al dente, about 10 minutes for bowtie pasta. A minute before the pasta is ready, put the sauté pan back over high heat. It will start to sizzle almost immediately. Pour a cup of the pasta water into the sauté pan and stir continuously.

When the pasta is al dente, drain and add to the sauté pan. Cook until the pasta water starts to evaporate and bubble at the bottom of the pan, about 3 minutes. Add the greens and herbs, one handful at a time, and toss to wilt. Continue adding until all are incorporated, then immediately remove from the heat. Spoon four equal portions into shallow bowls; shave Parmesan over the top, if desired, and serve immediately.

More Garden Recipes: Homegrown lettuces make wonderful salads, of course. Dress simply with olive oil, lemon juice, salt, and freshly ground black pepper. Lettuces can also be used to make a lettuce soup—sauté onions until cooked, add lettuce, add stock, and purée with some cream.

Pea Falafel

Falafel is traditionally made with mashed chickpeas; this version also uses garden peas. I learned it from my friend Mark, chef and owner of a popular Seattle restaurant, Spring Hill. We flattened Mark's back-yard years ago, and I have been growing produce for the restaurant ever since. Recently, he and I did a cooking demonstration—he cooked, I talked about how to grow the food. He took the glut of peas from the garden and made a spice-heavy fried falafel. Heaven. Plus it's a healthy dish. Try the falafel wrapped up in the Salt and Nigella Flatbread (page 83) and served with some pickled cucumbers and a spoonful of yogurt.

Serves 4

1 ¼ cup chickpeas

1 ¼ cup peas, shelled

½ large onion, chopped

¼ cup chickpea flour

½ teaspoon baking soda

1 teaspoon salt

1 teaspoon smoked paprika

1 teaspoon curry powder

1 teaspoon garam masala

¼ teaspoon freshly ground black pepper

¼ teaspoon cayenne

1 cup fresh herbs, such as lemon balm, mint, anise hyssop, lovage, tarragon, parsley, cilantro

½ lemon, zested and juiced

Olive oil for frying

The night before, soak the chickpeas on the counter in a bowl of cool water. Drain well in the morning and pat dry if still wet.

Bring a pot of salted water to a boil. Set up a water bath, filling a large bowl with cold water and ice. Set aside. Drop the shelled peas into the boiling water and cook until bright green and floating, 2 to 3 minutes. Drain and immediately drop them into the ice-water bath, halting the cooking process. Give them a stir to make sure they are cool, then drain and set aside.

Place the chickpeas and peas in the bowl of a food processor fitted with a steel blade. Add all other ingredients. Blend until broken down and well combined. The batter will be almost pastelike and should hold together. If it's too wet, add another spoonful of chickpea flour. Scrape it out of the processor bowl into another bowl and let stand for 30 minutes.

In a large sauté pan, add enough olive oil to cover the bottom of the pan and come up the sides a bit. Heat over medium heat. When the oil is hot, drop in small spoonfuls of the falafel batter and fry. The batter is quite soft, so do not move the cooking falafels around. Let one side get nice and golden brown before flipping them over. Continue frying on all sides until golden brown. Remove from the pan and drain on a paper bag. Repeat with the remaining batter. Serve immediately.

EDIBLE BLOSSOMS

Many plants produce flowers that are edible, often with a more muted version of the plant's leaf, stem, or root flavor. These blossoms can be harvested and eaten as well! They make a pretty presentation, and it's a good way to use all of the plant before pruning after bloom.

Anise hyssop: Gentle licorice flavor. Flower heads form a spike of many individual blossoms. To harvest, close your fist around the flower spike and pull the stem down to strip off the blossoms.

Arugula: Flouncy white petals that taste of spicy pepper and are a bit nutty.

Borage: Beautiful blue-violet flowers that taste mildly of cucumber.

Chamomile: Sweet, floral flavor. Best used in teas or cooked.

Chervil: Feathery white blossoms that are slightly fennel-tasting.

Chive: Spiky purple flowers that taste strongly of onion.

Dandelion: Bright yellow petals that taste rich and buttery.

Marjoram: Similar to oregano, these tiny flowers are best as garnish.

Nasturtium: Slightly peppery and brightly colored, these are great in salad.

Scented geranium: Tastes like the plant variety's particular scent and is wonderful candied for garnish.

Squash: These big orange flowers don't taste like much, but their size makes them perfect for stuffing and cooking. Make sure you harvest only male blossoms (with a stamen—trust me, it should be obvious) and leave the female blossoms to produce fruit.

Thyme: Tiny little flowers that are strongly flavored like thyme.

More Garden Recipes: Peas make a great filling; you can mash them to fill ravioli or savory tarts. Try replacing half of the ricotta in the filling for the Borage Zucchini Tart (page 101) with mashed peas. Whole peas are also wonderful served with long pasta noodles. Make a quick sauce with prosciutto and butter in a sauté pan, add the peas, then toss with pasta. Finish with fresh mint and a grate or two of lemon zest.

Seared Pork Chops and Fennel Blossoms with Fig-Lovage Relish

I love figs, and I have long been a fan of lovage, which deserves to be much more widely known. Lovage tastes like a stronger version of a celery leaf. As its flavor is more pronounced—a little goes a long way. I serve this relish with seared pork chops, but it would be great on most roasted meats or a fatty fish like black cod. The pork chops are lightly rubbed with fennel blossoms (which can be harvested from the wild in summer), crushed coriander seeds, and paprika. It's a nice smoky combination of flavors to play off the sweetness of the figs. Feel free to omit the rub entirely and simply season the pork with salt and pepper; it will be equally delicious.

Serves 4

Relish

    12 dried figs, Calimyrna or Black Mission
    4 tablespoons finely chopped lovage (about 12 large leaves)
    1 teaspoon sherry vinegar
    1 tablespoon olive oil

Rub

1 teaspoon fennel blossoms

½ teaspoon freshly ground coriander

½ teaspoon salt

½ teaspoon freshly ground black pepper

Pork Chops

2 tablespoons olive oil

½ tablespoon butter

4 pork chops, rib chop, bone-in

1 tablespoon vermouth

To make the relish, chop the figs into small dice. Add the lovage, sherry vinegar, and olive oil to the figs. Stir and set aside to macerate.

To make the rub, combine the fennel blossoms, coriander, salt, and pepper. Sprinkle the rub on both sides of each of the chops, and pat it in. You want a pretty thin sprinkling, not a thick layer, so use sparingly, but use it all.

To make the pork chops, heat the olive oil and butter in a large sauté pan over medium heat. When the butter is melted and bubbling at the edges and the pan is hot, add the pork chops. Let sear until golden brown. Don't move the chops around, just let them sit and color. After about 6 minutes, you can see that the sides of the chops are beginning to cook. Flip them over and cook until cooked through and firm, another 5 to 6 minutes. Remove the chops to a plate and let them rest. Return the pan to the stovetop and increase the heat to high. The brown bits in the pan will start to sizzle and burn. Splash in the vermouth and quickly scrape loose all the bits. Cook for 1 minute more, then remove from heat.

To serve, place one pork chop per person on a dinner plate and garnish with a spoonful of the relish. Distribute pan juices evenly over the chops and serve immediately.

More Garden Recipes: Lovage is a natural accompaniment to shellfish. Steam a big pot of clams or mussels and add lovage when you add the shellfish. Lovage is also wonderful with eggs; for a healthy breakfast, soft-boil an egg and mash it onto a piece of toast, then garnish with a chopped lovage leaf and salt.

Thyme-Roasted Chicken Legs with Charred Onions

Inevitably, if I roast a chicken, the first piece I grab is the leg. It is often the case that I miss out, if I'm being polite to guests and letting them choose first. My friend Michelle solves this conundrum in her own family by purchasing an extra package of legs every time she roasts a chicken. Brilliant! Thyme is liberally added to both the chicken and onions in this recipe, but truly the beauty lies in the roasting. The chicken is started at a very high temperature. After twenty minutes, the legs are cooked slowly at a lower temperature for nearly an hour and come out of the oven almost like a "confit"—crispy outside, succulent inside. The result is a simple but homey dish of sweet onions and crispy chicken. As thyme is a hardy herb, this dish can be made well into the winter with thyme from the garden.

Serves 4

    8 chicken legs
    Salt
    2 onions, peeled and cut into half moons or rings of
    medium thickness
    3 tablespoons olive oil
    6 tablespoons chopped thyme, divided, plus more for garnish
    ½ teaspoon freshly ground black pepper
    1 lemon, zested

Prepare chicken legs by salting liberally at least an hour before cooking, and up to a day ahead. Store in a resealable plastic bag or plastic wrap and refrigerate until ready to use.

Preheat the oven to 450°F. In a large bowl, combine the onions, olive oil, and 3 tablespoons of the thyme and toss to coat. Spread the onions in an even layer on a large sheet pan. In the same bowl, combine the remaining thyme, 1 teaspoon salt, pepper, lemon zest, and the chicken legs. Toss to coat, rubbing some of the seasoning under the skin of the legs. Lay the legs directly on top of the onions, making sure the legs don't touch or overlap.

Place the sheet pan in the oven and roast for 20 minutes. Without opening the oven door, reduce the heat to 350°F and bake for 45 minutes to 1 hour, until the legs are golden brown and wrinkled. Check the pan every 15 minutes; if the onions along the edges are turning too black, toss as needed.

Remove the pan from the oven and transfer the onions to a large platter. Set the legs on top of the onions and garnish with a pinch of fresh thyme if desired. Serve immediately.

More Garden Recipes: Thyme is a great partner to lemon. Steep a sprig of thyme in lemonade or make a hot tea of thyme and lemon slices with honey. You can also make just the onions from this dish and bake them on a square of puff pastry for a quick party appetizer. Thyme infuses well; try substituting thyme for the anise hyssop in the Anise Hyssop Ice Cream (page 108) and serve with a bowl of berries.

Borage Zucchini Tart

This tart is made in stages, but it's worth the extra time. Using store-bought puff pastry, the tart is layered with borage-scented ricotta cheese and sautéed zucchini, then topped with a lattice of zucchini slices. Laticework takes time, so if you prefer not to fuss with it, simply layer zucchini in a row across the tart. Borage has a very distinct cucumber-like flavor and pairs nicely with zucchini. It's a great way to make use of a prolific container plant. If you are so inclined, you can make just

*the borage-ricotta mixture and serve a big spoonful over some pasta
dressed in olive oil. The cheese may also be used on crostini as an
appetizer or as filling in homemade ravioli. The tart can be made a
day ahead, wrapped loosely in parchment paper and refrigerated until
ready to serve.*

Serves 4

> Flour, for dusting
> 1 sheet puff pastry
> 2 large zucchini
> 1 tablespoon butter
> 1 tablespoon olive oil
> ½ onion, finely chopped
> Salt
> 1 cup ricotta
> 30 borage leaves, chopped fine
> 1 lemon, zested
> 2 tablespoons grated Parmesan
> ½ teaspoon freshly ground black pepper
> 1 egg yolk, beaten

To prepare the pastry shell, lightly dust a countertop with flour and roll out the puff pastry dough until it is half its original thickness—about an 11-by-11-inch square. Make three folds along each side of the dough, $1/_4$-inch wide, folding toward the center of the dough to form a wall of puff pastry. This wall will contain the filling. Press together firmly at the corners. Don't worry if your pastry isn't a perfect square; the dough will puff up in baking and these little imperfections will not show. Move the tart shell to a sheet pan and freeze until ready to use.

For the lattice top, slice one zucchini lengthwise on the thinnest setting of a mandoline, or using a knife, cut lengthwise into very thin strips. Set the strips on a cooling rack set over a sheet pan and salt lightly; this helps remove some moisture from the zucchini.

While the zucchini strips are draining, chop the remaining zucchini into small, even dice. Heat the butter and olive oil in a large sauté pan over medium-high heat. When the butter is melted, add the onions and cook until soft and translucent, about 8 to 10 minutes. Add the diced zucchini and a pinch of salt and sauté until the zucchini is just cooked through, about 4 minutes. Remove from the heat and spread the mixture on a sheet pan in a thin layer to cool.

In a small bowl, stir together the ricotta, borage, lemon zest, Parmesan, and pepper until well combined.

Press the zucchini strips between layers of kitchen towels or paper towels to remove any excess moisture.

Preheat the oven to 375°F.

To assemble the tart, take the pastry shell from the freezer. Spread the ricotta over the bottom of the shell. Evenly distribute the sautéed zucchini-onion mixture over the ricotta. Lay the zucchini slices across the tart, from top to bottom, overlapping the layers slightly. Working perpendicular to this layer, lay zucchini slices left to right. Make a latticework pattern by lifting every other row of zucchini running top to bottom and tucking the new horizontal slices over and under. Weave the strips across the entire tart, tucking under or cutting the edges so they do not hang over the tart walls.

When the lattice is complete, brush the entire top of the tart with the egg yolk. Bake until puffed up and golden brown, 40 to 45 minutes. Serve hot or at room temperature.

More Garden Recipes: Borage flowers make a lovely garnish for cocktails and summertime drinks. Young borage leaves can be torn and added to salads, imparting a soft cucumber flavor. For a light summer salad, sliver borage leaves and toss them with some steamed shrimp, lemon juice, and avocado.

Lemon Trout with Dandelion Greens

Whole fish can sometimes be intimidating, but trout cooks quickly and tastes great. No need to clean anything—commercial trout comes scaled and gutted already. I learned this wholesome and healthy recipe from my friend Jaime years ago; it has been a standard of mine ever since.

Whole trout is cooked quickly under the broiler and served topped with a salad of dandelion greens and almonds. The dandelion greens are quite bitter, but work well with the subtle fish. They are also very healthy for you; ounce for ounce, they have more vitamin A, iron, and calcium than broccoli. Harvest new dandelion growth in spring; older, bigger leaves are too tough and woody, and their flavor is harsh.

Serves 2

- 1 garlic clove, peeled
- 1 handful sliced almonds
- 2 handfuls dandelion greens, coarsely chopped
- 1 lemon, zested, then sliced
- 1 tablespoon olive oil
- Salt and freshly ground black pepper
- 1 whole trout

Preheat the broiler and raise a rack to the highest position in your oven.

In the bowl of a mortar and pestle, mash and grind the garlic clove. When the oils have covered the walls of the mortar, remove and discard the garlic flesh. Add the almonds to the bowl and grind until they are broken up into smaller pieces. Add the dandelion greens and lemon zest and mash all the ingredients together until combined. The mixture will look a little bit like a salad and a little bit like a pesto. Inconsistency in the size of the leafy bits is perfect. Add the olive oil and a pinch of salt and give it one last stir with the pestle. Set aside.

Meanwhile, season the trout on both sides and inside the belly with salt and pepper. Insert several lemon slices into the belly of the trout. Place on a sheet pan and lightly coat the trout with a drizzle of olive oil to prevent sticking. Place the sheet pan directly under the broiler, and broil on one side until the skin starts to shrivel and char, 4 to 5 minutes. Take out the pan and flip the trout with a spatula. Return to the broiler and broil the other side until charred and cooked through, 4 to 5 minutes.

Place the broiled trout on a platter and spoon the dandelion salad over it. Serve immediately.

More Garden Recipes: Dandelions are a great green for adding to your salad, but use them sparingly so they don't overpower the other flavors. Try making a dandelion pesto with crushed garlic and pine nuts. Dandelion greens can also be used as a filling for the Pea Vine Dumplings (page 84).

Sweets

Chamomile and Coconut Granola

My friend Lynda works as a cheese maker at a goat dairy. Last summer I got to spend a few days out in farm country with her, and every morning for breakfast I had a deep bowl of her perfect goat milk yogurt topped with spoonfuls of her homemade granola and a drizzle of honey. Her granola has no added butter or sugar, so it's not gooey-crunchy like most granola, but it does have toasty, flaky bits like coconut, oats, and almonds. The flavor is intensified with some chamomile buds and sesame seeds. After trying this, you'll never think of granola in the same way again.

Makes 6 servings

   1 cup rolled oats
   1 cup sliced almonds

1 cup raw, unsweetened coconut flakes

¼ teaspoon salt

1 teaspoon crushed dried chamomile buds

1 tablespoon untoasted sesame seeds

1 tablespoon flaxseed meal

Preheat the oven to 350°F. Place all ingredients on a sheet pan and stir to combine. Place in the oven and toast for 5 minutes. Remove the pan from the oven and toss, redistributing granola into a single layer. Toast until the coconut flakes are golden brown, another 3 to 4 minutes. Serve by the handful over a bowl of plain yogurt with a drizzle of honey and some fresh fruit. Cooled leftover granola can be stored in the pantry, in a sealed container, for about 3 weeks.

More Garden Recipes: Chamomile is a great fit with oats. Try some in your oatmeal, add some to your favorite oatmeal cookie recipe, or toss some crushed buds into a topping for fruit crisp.

Rosy Strawberries with Buttermilk Cake

Rose geranium is an easy-to-grow flower that is best used in sweet recipes and desserts. It imparts a distinctive flavor to a dish, and I love its floral scent with strawberries. In this recipe, ripe berries are sim-ply macerated with some sugar and finely chopped *rose geranium leaves. On the side, I like to serve this easy buttermilk cake. The sweet rosy sauce can also be eaten on its own, spooned over vanilla ice cream, or just as is, maybe with a splash of cream on top.*

Serves 4

Strawberries

1 pint strawberries, hulled and quartered

¼ cup sugar

5 large rose geranium leaves, chopped fine

Cake

- 1 cup whole wheat pastry flour
- 1 cup all-purpose flour
- 1 teaspoon baking powder
- 1 teaspoon baking soda
- ½ teaspoon salt
- 1 cup buttermilk
- 1 teaspoon vanilla extract
- ¼ pound butter (1 stick), at room temperature
- 1 cup sugar
- 2 large eggs
- Powdered sugar (optional)

Combine the strawberries, sugar, and rose geranium leaves in a small bowl and let stand for thirty minutes before serving.

Preheat the oven to 350°F. Butter a 9-inch cake pan and set aside. Combine the flours, baking powder, baking soda, and salt in a small bowl and set aside. Combine the buttermilk and vanilla in a separate bowl and set aside.

Using an electric mixer, cream the butter and sugar until well incorporated, about 5 minutes. The mixture should be light and fluffy. Add the eggs, one at a time, mixing until well incorporated, scraping the sides of the bowl. Add half of the flour mixture and stir until just combined. Add the buttermilk mixture and stir until well combined. Add the remainder of the flour mixture and stir until just combined. Pour the dough into the cake pan and bake for 30 to 40 minutes, or until a toothpick inserted in the middle comes out clean.

Cool the cake on a cooling rack and dust with powdered sugar, if desired. Serve with a generous spoonful of macerated berries.

More Garden Recipes: Rose geranium can be steeped in cream for an ice cream base or a scented whipped cream. Try blending leaves with milk and strawberries for a quick, nutritious breakfast smoothie.

Anise Hyssop Ice Cream

I fell in love with the conical shape of the purple anise hyssop flower at a farmers' market years ago. Taking a bite, I fell in love a second time with the flavor. Having no idea what to do with this new herb—part licorice, kind of minty—I steeped it in some milk and made ice cream. It quickly became one of my favorites; I make this often and pair it with berries and cakes instead of the usual suspect, vanilla.

Makes about 2 pints

> 1½ cups whole milk
>
> ½ cup sugar
>
> 10 anise hyssop leaves
>
> 3 egg yolks, plus 1 whole egg
>
> 1½ cups heavy cream

In a medium saucepan, heat the milk, sugar, and anise hyssop leaves over medium heat until hot but not boiling. Remove from the heat and let steep for about 30 minutes, or until the flavor tastes good to you. Return the mixture to medium heat and warm through.

In a glass bowl, whisk the egg yolks and egg until well combined. Add one ladleful of the warm milk mixture to the eggs, whisking continuously. Add another ladleful and whisk until well combined. (You are tempering the eggs slowly to a warm liquid so that you do not cook them when you add them to the saucepan.)

Pour the egg mixture into the saucepan with the milk mixture and cook over medium heat, stirring continuously, for about 8 minutes. Be careful not to boil. Cook, stirring often, until the custard lightly coats the back of a wooden spoon. Remove the custard from the heat and strain into a large mixing bowl. (Straining will remove any curdled egg as well as the anise hyssop leaves.) Add the heavy cream and stir to combine.

Lay plastic wrap directly on the surface of the custard and refrigerate until cold, at least 4 hours or overnight. Freeze according to the manufacturer's instructions in an ice cream maker, occasionally scraping the sides of the bowl, until creamy and frozen. Store the ice cream in an airtight container in the freezer until ready to serve.

More Garden Recipes: Add a few anise hyssop leaves to a grain or legume salad for a fresh flavor combination. Anise hyssop is also wonderful in herbal sun teas.

SUGAR PETALS

I find that although some edible flowers are tasty, most petals don't taste like much of anything. When I have a plant that produces flowers and I want to fancy up desserts or platters of fruit, I make sugared petals and use them as small garnishes. You can employ this same method with herb leaves. Sugared mint, anise hyssop, and even sage are delicious touches that are not only flavorful but lovely to look at.

It is quite easy, but tedious work to sugar petals and leaves, so be prepared to practice your patience! Prepare your space. Set up a cooling rack and a large plate. The cooling rack will be used to dry the petals once they're sugared. The sheet pan will collect all of the excess sugar. You'll also need tweezers.

Cut stems from the plant and gently break apart the flower head to release individual petals. In a small bowl, beat one egg white, then thin with a splash of water. Pick up each petal with the tweezers (so your fingers don't get stick to the petal). Using a pastry brush or small paintbrush, brush the petal with a *thin* coat of egg wash. For large leaves, you can lay them in the palm of your hand when brushing. Be sure to coat both sides. (And *no*, you can't get lazy and just dip the leaf or petal—the coating will be far too thick.) When both sides are brushed with the egg white wash, hold the leaf or petal with the tweezers and sprinkle sugar on each side, holding it over the sheet pan so any excess sugar can be reused. Set on the cooling rack to dry.

Here is a short list of pretty petals and flavorful leaves to sugar:

Anise hyssop leaves	**Nasturtium**
Lemon verbena	**Rose geranium**
Mint leaves	

Chocolate Lavender Tart

This tart is utterly dense and rich—a very small slice is plenty. It's a great dessert to make for dinner party guests, as it easily serves twelve to twenty people. A simple ganache is made by melting chopped chocolate into milk. You choose how subtle or forthright the flavor should be by controlling how long to infuse the cream with lavender buds. (I like the lavender flavor to really shine through, so I steep flowers in the cream for about 40 minutes.) You must prebake the tart shell for this recipe, so this is a recipe to make in stages by baking the shell a day in advance. This chocolate tart will hold at room temperature, or wrapped tightly in the fridge, for several days.

Serves 12 to 20

Tart Shell

- 1 cup all-purpose flour
- 1 cup whole wheat pastry flour
- 1 teaspoon salt
- 1 teaspoon sugar
- ½ pound (2 sticks) chilled unsalted butter, cut into small cubes
- 8 tablespoons ice water

Filling

- 1 cup heavy cream
- 1½ tablespoons lavender buds
- 10 ounces bittersweet chocolate, chopped very fine
- 3 egg yolks

To make the tart shell, put the flours, salt, and sugar in the bowl of a food processor fitted with a steel blade, and pulse once or twice to combine. Add the butter and pulse until the dough just comes together in large crumbs—be careful not to overprocess.

With the machine running, slowly add the ice water, 1 tablespoon at a time, until the dough is just combined and comes together in two or three large portions. You may not need all of the water to do this. This takes about 8 to 10 seconds; be careful not to overprocess.

Turn the dough out onto a countertop and divide in half, pressing each half into two flat round disks, each about 6 inches in diameter. Be careful not to work the dough. Wrap each piece tightly in plastic wrap and refrigerate for at least 2 hours.

When ready to use, remove the dough from the fridge. Lightly flour a work surface. Using a rolling pin, roll out the dough into about a 10-inch round (be sure to rotate the dough and flip it over, rolling both sides). Keep the work surface lightly floured so the dough does not stick.

Fold the round in half and place over a 9-by-11-inch tart pan with a removable bottom, (with the folded edge running down the middle of the pan). Unfold the disk so it hangs over the edge of the tart pan. Press it gently into the tart pan, being careful not to stretch it too thin. Turn any overhanging crust under and press it into the walls of the pan. Run a rolling pin over the top of the pan, pressing down to level out the top of the shell. Pierce the bottom of the tart shell with a fork in several places. Freeze for 30 minutes before baking.

Preheat the oven to 350°F. Remove the pan with the tart shell from the freezer and line the inside of the shell with parchment paper. Put pie weights or beans on the parchment paper, pressing into the corners.

Bake on the center rack for 30 minutes. Remove the pie weights and parchment and bake until toasty brown, another 10 to 15 minutes. Remove the tart shell from the oven, let cool, and set aside until ready to use.

To make the filling, heat the cream and lavender over medium-low heat. When warm, set aside to infuse. If the cream cools, heat up again slightly and continue to let steep. The lavender should steep in the warm cream from 20 to 40 minutes, depending on how strong a flavor you're after.

Meanwhile, place the chocolate in a bowl. In another bowl, whisk the egg yolks until smooth.

When the cream is done steeping, strain out the buds and return the cream to medium-low heat. Heat until it just begins to steam, about 2 minutes. Slowly add spoonfuls of cream to the eggs while whisking vigorously. This will temper the eggs so they don't cook too quickly and curdle. Continue whisking as you finish adding all of the cream to the eggs. Once all the cream is added and well blended with the yolks, set a strainer over the bowl of chocolate and pour in the hot cream and egg yolk mixture.

Using a rubber spatula, fold the hot cream around the chocolate bits. Give the chocolate a stir every few minutes to melt it completely. (If all of the chocolate does not melt, and the chocolate is cool, you can set it briefly over a double boiler with simmering water to heat slightly.)

Pour the filling into the cooled pie shell and set aside to firm up, for 1 to 2 hours. Serve the tart at room temperature. Leftovers can be wrapped tightly and refrigerated for several days.

More Garden Recipes: Lavender can be crushed up and combined with other herbs like rosemary and thyme to use as a dry rub for meat. Try adding it to Crispy Marjoram Potatoes (page 89) along with the marjoram. Or try steeping lavender buds in milk for ice cream.

Blackberry Peach Crisp with Lovage

Lovage is an herb that is typically used in savory recipes, but the aromatic seeds also work in sweet desserts. In particular, the spicy note pairs well with stone fruits, like the peaches in this crisp. Baked fruit crisps are one of the simplest and quickest desserts to make. The combination of peaches and blackberries, along with the lovage seeds, make this a perfect seasonal dessert to serve in late summer. Serve the crisp with ice cream or whipped cream on the side. Any leftovers can be refrigerated or covered tightly in parchment paper and held at room temperature.

Serves 4 to 6

Filling

1½ pounds peaches, cut into large chunks

1½ pounds blackberries

1 cup sugar

Topping

½ cup whole wheat pastry flour

½ cup rolled oats

½ cup brown sugar

¼ cup coarsely chopped pecans

1½ teaspoons ground cinnamon

1 teaspoon lovage seeds, gently crushed

¼ teaspoon freshly grated nutmeg

¼ teaspoon salt

6 tablespoons cold unsalted butter

Preheat the oven to 350°F.

In a large bowl, toss the peaches, berries, and sugar. Pour into a large baking dish and set aside.

To make the topping, combine the flour, oats, brown sugar, pecans, cinnamon, lovage, nutmeg, salt, and butter. Using your fingertips, massage the mixture together until it forms a coarse crumb and larger clumps. When the butter is massaged in and the topping comes together, spread evenly over the fruit.

Bake on the center rack until the crisp is golden brown with juices bubbling around the sides, 40 to 45 minutes.

More Garden Recipes: Lovage seeds are a great spice for your cupboard. You can grind lovage and use is as a rub for grilled or roasted meats. Lovage can take the place of fennel seeds in most recipes.

Blackberry Buttermilk Ice Cream

This blackberry buttermilk ice cream is nearly guilt free, as it uses low-fat buttermilk and a minimum of sugar. Be sure to rinse off city-picked blackberries before you use them (see Blackberry Jam, page 120). I learned how to adjust the freezing temperature of ice cream years ago from my chef friend, Thierry. He makes killer sorbets, and I could never figure out how. A bit of booze raises the freezing temperature of the mix and therefore makes it seem a bit smoother and less icy. A good tip to keep in your pocket.

1 pint

½ pound blackberries (about 2 cups)
¼ cup sugar
1 cup low-fat buttermilk
1 teaspoon vodka

In a bowl, macerate the blackberries and sugar for 30 minutes on your countertop. When juicy, purée in a blender with the buttermilk and vodka. Pour through a fine mesh sieve to strain out all the blackberry seeds and hairs.

Add the mixture to an ice cream maker and freeze according to the manufacturer's instructions, occasionally scraping the sides of the bowl, until creamy and frozen. Store ice cream in an airtight container in the freezer until ready to serve.

More Garden Recipes: Try the crisp or blackberry jam for more blackberry ideas.

Lemon Verbena Ice

In the heat of summer, there's nothing like an icy, refreshing treat or beverage. Lemon verbena is at its best in midsummer—this plant loves the heat. It also tends to be prolific and will put on growth quickly once it is cut. This recipe is quite simple and can be used with a number of herbs. It is essentially an infused simple syrup, frozen with a bit of wine. To make an icy granita, you must rake ice crystals through the mixture every 15 minutes or so. This results in a very icy dessert, not nearly as smooth as a sorbet. You can also use the granita in beverages. Add some to a glass and splash with some gin and fizzy soda for an evening cocktail. Add some fresh lemon verbena leaves as garnish.

Serves 4 to 6

  2 cups water
  2 cups sugar
  20 to 30 lemon verbena leaves
  1 cup light, crisp white wine, such as sauvignon blanc
  1 tablespoon lemon juice

In a medium saucepan, bring the water, sugar, and lemon verbena leaves to a boil. Stir to dissolve the sugar, then remove from the heat and let the lemon verbena steep. When the water is cool, taste to make sure the lemon verbena flavor is nice and strong. If not, add a fresh round of leaves, bring to a boil, and steep some more. When the flavor is right, add the wine and pour the liquid into a shallow baking dish. Place in the freezer. After 20 minutes, check to see whether the liquid is partially frozen. Pull a fork through, raking up any ice crystals, and return to the freezer. Wait 15 minutes and repeat. Continue doing this until the entire mixture is flaky and frozen.

More Garden Recipes: Lemon verbena is commonly used in teas and is delicious steeped on its own with honey. Its leaves may be steeped in cream for ice cream or custards. This herb also pairs nicely with lamb and other gamey meats. Add chopped leaves to marinades for lamb chops or steaks. Lemon verbena can be used as a substitute for lemon zest in some recipes.

WATER-BATH CANNING 101

This is a step-by-step guide to water-bath canning at home. There are a few options to choose from, but all work well. Be sure to set up your jars and workspace beforehand so you can establish a rhythm. Also, be mindful of the processing times given in each recipe.

Cleaning the Jars

Wash the jars and lids in hot soapy water and set them to dry completely on a rack or a clean dish towel.

Preparing the Jars

Glass jars and lids do not need to be sterilized before use if your foodstuffs will be processed for more than 10 minutes in a boiling water bath or pressure canner. If jar-processing time is 10 minutes or less, jars must be sterilized before filling. Do this by placing the jars in a canning pot, filling with water, and bringing the water to a simmer. Hold the jars in water until ready to use. Conversely, I always hold just-washed jars in a 225°F oven until ready to use. This is not recommended by the USDA, but I'm still alive to give you the option.

Filling the Jars

All canned goods will need headspace to allow for expansion of the food and to create a vacuum in cooling jars. As a general rule, leave ¼ inch of headspace on all jams and jellies and ½ inch of headspace on all whole fruits. When using whole fruits, release air bubbles in just-filled jars by tapping the jar on the counter or by inserting a wooden chopstick or skewer into the jar and gently stirring the fruit. When placing lids and rings on canning jars, do not overtighten the rings. Secure just until the rings have tension and feel snug. Overtightening will not allow air to vent from the jars—a crucial step in canning.

Heating the Canning Pot

Fill your canning pot or a deep stockpot half full of water and heat to a low boil. Hold the liquid on a very low boil until ready to use.

Filling the Canning Pot

If using a canning pot, place the prepared jars of food on the rack in the canner. Do not stack, as you need to allow for circulation of water for proper sealing. Lower the jars into the canning pot and add enough water to cover the jar tops by an inch or more. Cover the pot and return to a boil. *Processing times begin once the canning-pot water is brought back up to a boil.* This can take as long as 15 minutes, so be sure to keep an eye on your pot and a timer nearby. You may also use a deep stockpot (best only in small-batch preserving) by lining the bottom of the pot with a dish towel and placing jars on top. This helps keep jars from clanging around on the bottom of the pot or tumbling over onto their sides. This form of canning is not universally recommended or endorsed by the USDA, but I have seen plenty of farmers and European country folk use this old-school technique, and I've adapted their laissez-faire ways.

Removing Sealed Jars

Using a jar lifter or a set of kitchen tongs, remove jars from the canner when the processing time has elapsed. (Remember, processing times begin once the canning-pot water is brought back up to a boil.) Set the jars aside on a folded towel to cool. Make sure you *do not press* on the tops and create an artificial seal.

Knowing When Jars are Sealed

You'll hear the sound of can tops popping shortly—a sign that a secure seal has been made. Once the jars are cool, check the seal by removing the outer ring and lifting the jar by holding only the lid. If it stays intact, you have successfully canned your food. If the seal is loose or broken, you can reprocess in the water bath within twenty-four hours. Be sure to use a new lid, and check the jar rim for cracks or nicks and replace if necessary. Or you can refrigerate the jar immediately and use within three weeks.

Labeling and Storage

Once cool, label all jars with date and contents. Successfully sealed jars should be stored in a cool, dark place such as a cupboard. Officially, canned goods keep for up to a year, but I have let them go a bit longer with little effect.

Rose Hip and Apple Butter

Harvested in midsummer, these rosy fruits are one of my favorite wild foods to collect. Rose hips are quite fibrous, so they take a fair amount of work to prepare for use in recipes. Fruit butters can take a long time to cook, and require careful watching and stirring. Worth the effort, this butter has subtle but inimitable rose fragrance and takes apple butter from a familiar comfort food to something sublime.

Makes 5 half-pint jars

> 2 pounds rose hips
> 1½ pounds tart apples, scrubbed and cut into 1-inch pieces
> 3 cups sugar
> 1 lemon, juiced, halves reserved

Cut the stems and ends from the rose hips and rinse. Add the rose hips to a large saucepan and barely cover with water. Bring to a boil, then let simmer until soft, 30 to 45 minutes. Run the rose hips through a food mill, reserving the pulp. This will separate the skin and most of the seeds and hairs from the fruit; it may take a few passes. Place the rose hip pulp in a fine mesh strainer set over a bowl and push the purée through, using a rubber spatula. This will catch any additional hairs or seeds.

Place the apples in a large stockpot and add enough water to just cover. Over medium to medium-high heat, bring to a simmer. Cook until the fruit is soft and you can mash it with the back of a spoon.

Working in batches, put the apples in a blender (only half full at a time, as hot liquids expand) and purée. Set a fine mesh strainer over the pot and sieve the apple purée back into the pot. Add the rose hip purée, sugar, and lemon juice and halves, and return the mixture to medium heat.

Cook over medium to medium-low heat, stirring continuously every few minutes, taking care not to let the fruit butter burn. If it is too hot and sticking to the bottom of the pot, lower the heat. The butter is done when you place a small spoonful on a cool plate and no liquid separates out from the solid to create a ring around it. This can take anywhere from 1 to 2 hours.

When the fruit butter has cooked to a consistency of your liking, remove the lemon halves. Pour the butter into glass jars. It will keep, refrigerated, for several weeks.

More Garden Recipes: Rose hips can be cooked down to a purée and sweetened all on their own—the rosy flavor is more pronounced. Sweetened rose hip purée can be used as an accompaniment to cheese plates, as a thin layer in the bottom of sweet fruit tarts, or as a condiment for roasted pork.

Nasturtium "Capers"

All parts of the nasturtium plant are edible—vine, leaf, flower, and seed. The seeds, when young, look like small nutmegs, with slightly wrinkled and creviced skins. Harvest them when the seeds are about the size of a pea. When harvested young, nasturtium seeds can be brined (soaked in a salt solution) or pickled with vinegar, much as you would a caper. Use in pastas or salads for a crispy pickled bite. Both brined and pickled seeds keep in the refrigerator. Pickled seeds are best used within three weeks; after that they tend to break down slightly and turn mushy. Like true capers, these are made in small batches, as the seeds tend to mature in cycles.

Makes ½ cup

> ½ cup nasturtium seeds
> 1 teaspoon coriander seeds
> 1 teaspoon mustard seeds
> 3 whole cloves

½ teaspoon salt

½ cup rice wine vinegar

2 tablespoons sugar

In a pint jar, place the nasturtium, coriander, and mustard seeds and the cloves and salt, and set aside. In a small pan over high heat, heat the rice wine vinegar and sugar until the sugar is dissolved and the vinegar is just boiling. Pour the hot vinegar into the jar. Let cool to room temperature. Secure the lid on the jar and refrigerate. Let the "capers" pickle for at least a day before eating.

More Garden Recipes: You can vary the spices in the pickling mixture. Try a garlic clove, red chili flakes for some heat, or a few slices of fresh gingerroot.

Blackberry Jam

Blackberries are everywhere come August, so it is smart to keep a bowl in your car so you can pull over and pick at a moment's notice. When foraging blackberries from the side of the road, soak them briefly before eating. Fill a deep bowl with cool water and pour them in gently, stirring them slightly in the water. This will also release any bugs or spiders and hairs. Pour off the top layer of debris before you drain the berries completely. Preserving berries is a great way to stock your pantry and extend the season. This recipe is for a simple jam, but you can easily cook it down for a shorter time and make a syrup instead.

Makes 4 half-pint jars

2 pounds cleaned blackberries

3 cups sugar

1 lemon, cut in half

Put the berries and sugar in a large saucepan. Squeeze juice from the lemon halves into the pan and add both halves to your pot. (This introduces natural pectin to your jam, which will help the jam to set.)

Set over medium heat. Cook until the berries release their juice and are starting to break down, about 20 minutes. Remove from heat, cover, and refrigerate overnight.

In the morning, put a plate in the freezer. You will use this to check the set of your jam.

Place the saucepan on medium-low heat and cook the berries until broken down, about 20 minutes. Discard the lemon halves and any lemon seeds. Purée the blackberries in a blender until smooth. Set a fine mesh strainer over the jamming pot, and pour in the purée, straining out any seeds from the jam. Cook the jam over medium-low heat, stirring often, until the desired consistency is reached. You can check the set of your jam by placing a spoonful on the chilled plate. For jam, you want the spoonful of fruit to remain intact and the surface to wrinkle when you push it gently with your finger. Cooking time is typically 30 to 40 minutes. (To make blackberry syrup, cook for less time and remove from the heat when the purée cooks down to a loose sauce.) When the jam is done, pour it into preserving jars and process in a hot water bath for 5 minutes (see Water-Bath Canning 101 on page 116).

More Garden Recipes: To preserve berries in your freezer, lay the clean berries in a single layer on a sheet pan and freeze them individually. When they are frozen through, toss them in a resealable plastic bag and stockpile them for winter smoothies and pies.

Herby Simple Syrup

Simple syrup is quite simply equal parts water and sugar. Simple syrups are wonderful for infusions—any flavor can be added, from fresh herbs or flowers to dried spices or teas. Simple syrups can be brushed over cakes (try it with the Rosy Strawberries with Buttermilk Cake on page 106), added to fizzy water for a cocktail with bit of sweetness, or tossed with fresh fruit as a flavor layer. They are a gentle way to add just a hint of something herby. Use any herb you like. Lavender goes well with gin and can be brushed on cakes, both vanilla and chocolate. Anise hyssop simple syrup is awesome with fresh berries. You can even try foraging for rose hips and turning them into a delicately flavored syrup to use on pancakes or over yogurt. All syrups can be frozen and turned into an icy granita for an easy dessert.

Makes 1 cup

> 1 cup sugar
>
> 1 cup water
>
> 3 tablespoons herbs, flowers, or spices

Add all ingredients to a small saucepan and bring to a boil. Remove the pot from the heat and let the herbs steep in the syrup. Check the flavor after 15 minutes and see whether it's to your liking. If so, strain out the solids and use the syrup as suggested. Store any leftover syrup in the refrigerator; it will keep for several weeks. If the flavor is not strong enough, continue to steep the herbs until you are satisfied. For a more intense infusion, strain the spent herbs and heat up the infused mixture again using a fresh batch of herbs, repeating the same process.

More Garden Recipes: Use extra herbs and flowers for Garden Tisanes (page 134) or herbal sun teas. You can also grind herbs in sugar or salt for garnish or a savory rub.

Chamomile Cordial

Cordials are essentially sweetened syrups infused with herbs, spices, or plants. They are simple to make and offer a wide range of flavors and essences to anyone willing to experiment. Cordials offer a perfect solution for a nonalcoholic "cocktail" that is nothing short of grown-up. For this syrup, you can use either fresh or dried chamomile flower heads.

Chamomile is known for its medicinal properties (and ability to soothe), and the sweet flavor from the flower heads also makes for a gentle summer drink. Add some syrup to fizzy water and serve over crushed ice. Add a splash of cognac—its gentle flavor won't overpower the floral note. This syrup is also delicious brushed onto a simple yellow or buttermilk cake.

Makes about 2 cups

> 2 tablespoons dried chamomile flowers (or 3 tablespoons fresh chamomile flower heads)
> 2 cups boiled water
> ¼ cup honey
> 2 cups seltzer water
> Cucumber slices, for garnish
> Cognac (optional)

Add the chamomile flowers to a muslin steeping bag or fine mesh tea strainer. (Chamomile seeds are quite small and thin, so be sure to use fine mesh so they don't escape and float in your syrup.) Steep in the boiled water until the liquid is stained yellow and perfumed, about 20 minutes. Press any reserved liquid out from the muslin bag and discard the solids. Add the honey and stir until dissolved. Refrigerate until cool.

Once the syrup is completely cooled, add crushed ice to a glass. For each serving, pour in about ½ cup of the chamomile cordial and top with ½ cup seltzer water. Garnish with a thin slice of cucumber. If you like, add a float of cognac and serve immediately.

Store the cordial in a clean jar or bottle, covered, in the fridge, where it will last for several weeks.

More Garden Recipes: Chamomile can be used in place of lovage seeds in the crisp topping for the Blackberry Peach Crisp with Lovage (page 112). Dried chamomile heads also make for a gentle tea.

Chapter 7

Do-It-Yourself Garden

Being crafty—making little pots of lip balm or mixing your own teas—is a fun way to incorporate more of the garden into your everyday life. It's also great practice in creative thinking. I have often sat in my garden and stared around at the plants, thinking hard about what I could make from the mini-farm I have nurtured. I love a good homemade anything—my cupboards are lined with flavored sugars, seasoned salts, crackers, and jams that I've made myself.

When I see something I like that seems as if it can be easily made, my first inclination is to think, "I can do that." Particularly products of the five-ingredients-or-less sort. Plenty of do-it-yourself projects can be inspired from the garden.

A few years ago I was staring out at my plants, brainstorming what I could do with them. I had five scented geranium plants at the time, and while I love to look at them, I'm more interested in growing things that produce for me in multiple ways. My friend and neighbor Ritzy was really into organic beauty products and living green. Her shelves were lined with them, and whenever I was over I'd go snooping and dab a little cream here or rub some oil there. It was luxurious, something I would never ever spend money on. Her influence plus my plants' vigor inspired me to make my own products. I started out with a simple facial toner. Toner may seem like a superfluous beauty aid, but it smells pretty and it has astringent qualities (which are great when you're working out in the sun and sweating all day). I don't *buy* toner. But if I have all the ingredients to make a little batch of something special, why not? And for the record, toner isn't just for the ladies. Men can also do with a little astringent on their skin each day.

This and many other garden projects can be inspired by what is mature and ready to be harvested in your garden. Often I find that a plant needs trimming when I have no obvious use for what I harvest. In those moments, I turn away from my meal preparations and look to my cupboards to see how I can preserve or use it in some way. Beauty products are easy to whip up, and they make great hostess gifts. You can also dry your herbs and make your own teas, rubs, and flavored salts. And once winter sets in and there is nary a plant in sight, these are all wonderful reminders that the summer sun will come again.

Here are some of my favorite DIY garden projects.

HERBAL APOTHECARY

Facial Toner

When I was little, my mom always had a huge bottle of witch hazel astringent in our bathroom cabinet. We used to moisten cotton balls and rub it across our skin in summer to cool ourselves down. I imagine my mom kept it around for its toning and tightening attributes. To this day, I love the smell of witch hazel. This toner was adapted from a great book, *Herbal Recipes for Vibrant Health* by Rosemary Gladstar, and can be used to remove any excess facial oil and tighten pores. Vinegar acts as a preservative, so this toner is shelf-stable. It should be noted that the toner will have a slight vinegar scent, but it is not offensive, nor does it linger. Witch hazel is used in equal proportions for its toning quality. I'm including my favorite herb mix, but feel free to vary the herbal components. The only *must* is that once introduced, your herbs should remain submerged in the vinegar at all times.

Flower & Mint Toner

    10 rose geranium leaves
    10 chamomile heads
    6 lemon balm leaves
    6 mint leaves
    1 cup organic apple cider vinegar
    1¼ cup witch hazel

Wash a glass pint jar in hot soapy water and dry. Tear and bruise the herbs and flowers and add them to the glass jar. Heat the vinegar until hot, but not boiling, then pour over flowers and herbs. Cover the jar tightly and store in a dark cupboard in the kitchen for 2 to 3 weeks. Make sure the herbs remain submerged.

After up to 3 weeks have passed, strain out the herbs. Add the witch hazel and stir to blend. Pour the finished toner into a small glass jar and use daily on just-washed skin.

Infused Oils

Infused oils, essential oils, solar-infused oils—these all fall under one umbrella wherein oil acts as a carrier for a plant's own oil and scent. Olive oil is used overwhelmingly in homemade infusions. Infused oils can be used on their own as either a skin moisturizer or a garnish on meals (no joke) or as a base for salves or medicinal oils. Infused oils should be stored in a cool, dark place—heat and light will affect the stability of the oil. Properly stored, they will last for weeks, if not years. Moisture is also a spoiler, so make absolutely certain your jars and tools are completely dry before bottling, and use only dry herbs.

HERB DRYING

Drying herbs (or most edibles for that matter) is a satisfying project and the perfect way to extend your harvest. Herbs put out growth quite quickly. Combine fast-growing plants with busy lifestyles, and many home gardeners find they aren't home enough to use fresh-cut herbs in time. These plants also do better when you are actively cutting from them and stimulating them to put on new growth. I often see herbs go to flower when they should be cut back and used in cooking instead. When your herbs are growing faster than you're able to incorporate them into your meals, it's time to turn to herb drying.

To dry out fresh herbs, choose a warm, dry place. Molds, bacteria, and yeast all thrive in moisture and can ruin herb-saving projects, so keep drying herbs free from excess moisture. As a general rule of thumb, cut herbs almost down to the root, making certain to leave some green leaves and room for them to continue growing. (General harvesting tips can be found in Chapter 3, What to Grow, For Real.) There are two methods for drying herbs: hanging or tray drying. For hanging herbs, tie the stems together and hang from a hook in the ceiling until dry. For tray drying, place the herb cuttings on a parchment-lined baking sheet and turn them occasionally so moisture does not collect under the leaves. Most herbs should dry out in four to six days. They are fully dry when they crumble easily to the touch.

There are two effective methods for making an infused oil. One is the quick and easy way that can be done in a day's time. This process heats herbs over low heat on the stovetop or in the oven, thereby releasing their oil and scent into the carrier oil. Another option is a sun infusion, wherein light and heat from the sun slowly warm your herbs over time and help to release their essential oils. If you have the time and the organizational skills, go with the sun infusion. These long, slow, low-maintenance infusions are considered the best.

For all infusions, make sure you start with very clean herbs. If your herbs or flowers have any soil or dust on them, submerge in a bowl of cool water to rinse. Press between layers of a towel to remove some moisture and lay out in a single layer on a drying rack until completely dried out. This can take several hours, so be sure to move the leaves around and make certain they are not overlapping.

Once herbs are dry, they tend to be quite delicate and may scatter easily when touched. To make sure I catch all the dehydrated leaves, seeds, or blossoms, I will often put the herbs in a large paper bag while still holding the tied stems. Suspending the stalks upside down, I shake the dried leaves into the bag, or pull the entire stem gently through my fist to strip them off. This technique helps to make sure that you're actually capturing all the leaves or seeds instead of spreading them all over the house! When the stems are free of all leaves, pour the leaves onto a clean counter (covered with paper towels or newspaper) or a sheet pan. Work to separate out any stems or dirt particles from the actual herb leaves. As leaves are much lighter then stems and dirt, you can blow ever so lightly on a small pile and they will sort themselves— the leaves moving away from the "breeze." Scoop up the clean leaves— or a dough scraper works awesomely, a spoon works too—add them to a glass jar, and store in your spice cupboard (which should be cool, dry, and far from any heat sources).

Some herbs dry better than others, of course. Here is a short list of herbs that are prolific and make good pantry stockers:

Lemon Balm	Rosemary
Lemon Verbena	Sage
Marjoram	Thyme
Mint	

Stovetop Infusion

1 cup olive oil
2 handfuls herbs or flowers

In small saucepan over very low heat, warm up the olive oil and herbs. Let steep for at least 2 hours and up to 8, stirring occasionally. The oil is done steeping when its scent is unmistakable. Using a fine mesh strainer, strain out all of the leaves and branches, pressing against them to release all the plant's oil into the infusion. Repeat the process using already-infused oil if a stronger scent is desired.

Store the oil, covered, in a cool dark cupboard until ready to use.

Sun Infusion

> 1 cup olive oil
> 2 handfuls herbs or flowers

Add the oil and herbs or flowers to a quart-size glass jar. Make sure all the plant material is submerged in the oil. Cover and place the jar in the sun, where it should steep for the better part of two weeks. Be sure to move it around to keep it in the sun during the day.

After two weeks, use a fine mesh strainer to strain out all of the leaves and branches, pressing against them to release all the plant oils into the infusion. Repeat the process using already-infused oil if a stronger scent is desired.

Lip Balm

Last spring I was at the Quillisascut Farm School in Eastern Washington, and we were thinking about all the great things we could make with herbs. In the midst of talking, Lora Lea excused herself from the table and came back with a big old jar of green oil. It was thyme-infused oil, and it was heavenly. We made lip balm immediately, and I was officially hooked on the process. Though it had always intimidated me in the past, it turns out to be pretty easy; all you need is infused oil and some beeswax. Beeswax can be found at most local co-ops or natural food stores. This is also a quick version for making a salve for cuticles or elbows. It smells so good, you may even want to eat it—but don't.

Thyme Lip Balm

> 2 big handfuls of thyme, thoroughly cleaned
> 1 cup olive oil
> 2 ounces beeswax, grated

In small saucepan over low heat, warm up the olive oil and herbs. Let steep for a few hours, stirring occasionally. The oil should turn green from the thyme leaves. Using a fine mesh strainer, strain out all of the leaves and stems.

Return the oil to low heat, add the beeswax, and stir until melted. Remove from the heat and beat the mixture with an electric mixer. This fluffs up the salve and makes it über-creamy.

When it is lighter green in color and increased in volume, place into small jars or tins. Let cool and cap snugly.

Basic Salve

Salves are quite similar to lip balms and vary only in their consistency. Lip balms require more beeswax so they will hold together firmly. Skin balms can remain slightly softer. Salves can be used for moisturizing or for their healing properties. Lavender is considered to have both emotional calming and skin-soothing qualities, and can be used on scratches, bug bites, or stings. Mint salve is stimulating and leaves you feeling alive and invigorated. Try any flower or herb you like, but I suggest keeping them as a single note—do not combine herbs and flowers in one infusion. Keep them separate and mix two infusions if desired. You have more flexibility if you reserve each infusion for an individual scent.

Herbal Salve

> 1 ounce beeswax
> ½ cup infused oil (see Infused Oils project on page 127)

Add the beeswax and infused oil to a small saucepan (that is used specifically for this purpose, otherwise the salve will pick up scents from other cooking) and heat over low heat until the beeswax is melted. Remove from the heat, pour into small jars or tins, and cover.

Herb Salts

A few years back, one of my gardens had a lovage plant that just exploded with seeds. I went down there late one summer day and found the entire plant had blossomed and gone to seed. Not wanting them to go to waste, I trimmed all the stems, took the seed-laden flower heads home, and dried them out on racks. That little adventure kept my spice cupboard stocked with lovage seeds for the entire year. (I still have some, in fact!) With the extra seeds, I made some savory salt, which friends have clamored for. I'm not sure if it is the heady and distinctive smell of the seeds or the idea that you can sprinkle the salt on anything savory, but this salt rub is a total winner.

Herb salts are excellent for that very reason: they are incredibly versatile. You can use them for salting meat, dressing salads, seasoning grains, and more. Salts can be mixed using any salt you prefer. I lean toward kosher salt, as it's coarse without being too crunchy and not as mineral-tasting as some of the sea salts can be. When using seeds, I prefer to smash and pulverize them in a mortar and pestle so they are wholly incorporated into the salt. With herbs or flowers, I just toss them with the salt to combine. It is good to note that salt acts as a preserving agent. Salt absorbs moisture—a risk factor for mold—from the herbs, so it should keep spoilage to a minimum.

Here are some good ideas from the garden; feel free to experiment with your own.

Blossom Salt

You will begin to notice that many herbs come to maturity about the same time, which means they will also blossom at the same time. Herbs that flower typically need to be cut back, but you may find that you won't always have an immediate use for them. When I know I won't have time to cook with them, I use the blossoms in an herbal salt. Chive and thyme flowers work in flavorful harmony together, so they are good companions. Chive blossoms have a strong onion flavor, so be sure to check the flavor after the salt sits for a few days.

> 2 tablespoons chive blossom
> 3 tablespoons thyme blossom
> ½ cup kosher salt

Strip any stems off the flowers and put them in a bowl. Add salt, stirring to incorporate. Add enough salt so it is at least in equal proportion to the blossoms. If the flavor is too strong, you may add some more salt to adjust the proportions to your liking.

Lovage Salt

This is a great way to use lovage seeds, as they have such a strong flavor. They do well when split and smashed, so give them a good turn with a mortar and pestle before mixing.

> 3 tablespoons dried lovage seed
> 1 cup kosher salt

With a mortar and pestle, crush and pulverize lovage seeds until split into at least a third of their original size. Add half the salt to the mortar and mix together, crushing some of the salt. Add the rest of the salt and stir with a rubber spatula to combine. Using a rubber spatula will help pick up any oils from the seed pressed into the mortar. Pour into a glass jar or small tin, cap snugly, and store in a cool, dark cupboard until ready to use.

Garden Tisanes

Tisane is another name for an herbal tea. When you have a small urban garden, teas are especially clever to make so that you can enjoy a little piece of your garden all year long. Often when I have plants that are not doing well, or leaves that are starting to turn, I will make a quick tisane and add some honey to it. Teas may offer healing properties, and different herbs are used for different reasons. Typically at home, however, I make a tisane out of whatever I have available and am in the mood for. Mint and anise hyssop are great for settling the stomach. Mint alone is energizing. Chamomile is calming.

Tisanes can be made with fresh or dried leaves. Dried leaves tend to be stronger. Plan on using 3 tablespoons of fresh herbs or flowers or 1 tablespoon dried for every cup of water.

Drying out your own herbs gives you versatile ingredients for homemade tea mixes. Store mixes in a glass jar in your cupboard or store individual dried plants and mix up a blend to order. Personally, I keep all of my herbs in separate jars and mix them on the spot, according to preference. Here are some great combinations for garden tisanes:

Anise hyssop + Mint

Anise hyssop + Lemon balm + Mint

Chamomile + Lavender

Chamomile + Lovage + Mint

Lavender + Mint + Rose geranium

Lavender + Lemon verbena

Lemon verbena + Rose geranium

Herb-Infused Spirits

Infusing alcohol with your own mix of herbs and spices is another idea to use any excess that the garden puts up. The high alcohol content of spirits acts as a preservative, thereby minimizing spoilage. You can infuse most spirits, but the clean, clear options are the best: vodka, gin, and light rum. Infused spirits from garden herbs make great holiday gifts. Stock up over summer; come winter, your friends will love you for it.

You can also infuse your spirits with a mixture of fruit and herbs. My good friends Luke and Sarah, owners of Oxbow Farms, are always infusing or blending something or another with their garden glut. Last year their plum tree produced far too much fruit for eating fresh, so they made plum- and chamomile-infused rum. They used the rum for sipping and the soaked fruit in an upside-down cake.

To make, add the herbs to a clean glass jar and bruise the leaves slightly with the handle of a wooden spoon to release some oils. Pour enough alcohol over them to just cover. Cap snugly, shake a few times, and store in a cool, dark cupboard. Spirit infusions need to be shaken a few times every day. After three days, taste and see whether the flavor is right or it should sit longer. A good flavor generally takes five to seven days to develop, but is completely up to you.

When the flavor is right, strain out the herbs and return the infused spirits to a sealable container. Store in a cool, dark cupboard until ready to use.

Herb and spirit combos to try:

Gin + Anise hyssop

Gin + Lovage

Gin + Mint

Rum + Chamomile

Vodka + Basil

Vodka + Lemon verbena

Creative Plant Labels

I am never quite sure why people spend money on little things they could make at home. Plant labels fall into this category (unless you're growing on a large scale and need them in bulk, in which case buying labels is the way to go.) Starts typically come with labels, but I prefer the garden to look more uniform, so I invest some time in the look and feel of my plant labels.

Seed-Starting Labels

Plant labels for seed starting are crucial. Small plants with only a few leaves are nearly impossible to identify. It takes years of growing the same thing over and over to be able to do that. Seeds are typically started in large seed trays with covers. Labels must be small enough so that they do not impede the cover, but large enough for you to get information on there. Also, because you are watering regularly, you need a material that will not break down easily (I learned this the first year, when I made labels from strips of a heavy cardstock paper—totally useless, as they were soon illegible.) I'm surprised no one on the market is making a label system for home growers. Having said that, I'm happy to report that through years of trial and error I have crafted a simple, cheap, and functional solution.

You will need transparent tape and bamboo skewers. To make each label, cut a skewer to approximately four-inch lengths. Cut tape to about the same length. Place the very top of the shortened bamboo skewer dead center in the tape (making sure the top of the skewer is flush with the top of the tape), then wrap the tape around, creating a little flag. The tape will adhere to itself and you can now write on either side with a ballpoint pen. I like to include the name of the seed and days to maturity (45 days, 65 days, and so on).

Collected Plant Labels

Small smooth rocks and river stones can be used in the urban garden as plant markers. Keep an eye out when you're out on a stroll or find yourself near a mountain stream. The smaller the better, as containers won't appreciate too much extra weight. You can write directly on these rocks with a permanent marker. In sun, the writing will fade over time, so you'll need to either rewrite the label every few months or cover with a quick coat of clear gloss paint.

Vintage Silverware

Years ago, my friend Marcus picked up a bunch of mismatched silverware for me when he was out "junking." He gave me big soup spoons and long butter knives with all sorts of vintage detailing—scrolls and hobnails. The metal was so worn, however, that I would never use them to eat; it caused a strange metallic reaction in my mouth. I relegated them to the back of my silver drawer and forgot about them.

A while later I found a blog post with exactly this kind of old silverware being used as tchotchkes. Those spoons had sweet expressions on them, but I thought the idea was perfect for an outdoor plant label that I could make myself. I gave it a go and loved the effect. You need only white glue and aged silverware for these labels. There are more craft-specific glues in the marketplace, but I always have this glue around for decoupage projects. I tried it and it worked, so I never explored any other more "professional" option. Take your spoon, knife, or fork and make a label from plain white paper that is small enough to fit along the length of the handle or in the bowl of the spoon. Write the plant name on this label—typically there isn't much room, so use a fine-tipped pen or marker. Attach the label to the handle or spoon bowl with white glue and let dry completely. Make a glue wash by mixing two parts white glue to about one part water. It should be thin, but tacky. Using a small paintbrush, brush over the label, being sure to cover it completely but lightly, so you don't have any lines. Let dry slightly and apply a new coat. Repeat for a third and final coat. If you really love this project and you want your labels to last a good long while, you can always finish by spraying with a clear UV- and water-resistant product. These are sold at housewares and hardware stores. When fully dry, stick the handle of the silverware in your potting soil, leaving the bowl of the spoon as the potting label.

Make-and-Bake Labels

This project is fun and scary, but requires procuring some materials to accomplish. It breaks my no-purchase rule, but it's worth it. You remember Shrinky Dinks, right? I *loved* them as a kid. I would painstakingly color in the lines and then bake them, watching them melt down into little plastic pictures. A few years ago, I was at a craft show and one of the vendors was making Shrinky Dink earrings. I stole her idea, used it for plant tags, and it turned out brilliantly. Shrinky Dink sheets can be purchased from most local toy stores or found online. The only trick is making a big enough label so that it ends up with large enough print to read. Typically, I cut the plastic for a plant label into a five-by-two-inch section. This will bake down to about a two-by-one-inch sign. I like the simplicity of black ink on the white background, but you can get creative and add color. As with the silverware labels, use a thin sharp marker or colored pencil for this project—it allows for precise lettering. You can also cut and bake just plain clear squares, then use a pencil to write the plant name. Over time, you can erase and reuse these labels.

You need to consider how exactly you will place the label in the plant container. You can lay the label directly on the soil. Consider punching a small hole in the top of your label before baking; after baking, you can run ribbon, string, or thread through this hole and tie it to the base of your plant. Or, make a small hole (using a small hole punch) on each side of the label, directly across from one another. After the label is baked, unfold two paper clips and bend the wire in half through the hole, on both sides of the label. This creates a tent post that you can pierce your soil with, in order to hold the label in place.

I do not like the look of plastic containers. They are awesome to have because they are cheap, but they are not awesome-*looking*, precisely because they are cheap. Whenever I use a plastic pot, I pick up a can of spray paint for a quick pot makeover. Spray paints come in a rainbow of colors and will contribute to the look and feel of your garden space. Choose any color you like—bright blues, yellows, and reds stand out nicely against the green of plants.

To paint your pot, work outside in a well-ventilated area (on a calm day), well away from buildings or cars. (Spray paint is quite light and has a tendency to disperse quickly through the air, and you don't want to paint a neighbor's car accidentally.) Lay down newspaper three times as wide as the pot to protect the ground or grass you're working on. Follow the directions on the can—hold it about six inches away from the pot and move steadily across the surface. I pivot the container on one end with my left hand while simultaneously spraying with my right. You need only spray the interior rim of the pot about three inches down. Soil will fill the rest of the pot's interior. While spraying, keep the can at a distance of a few inches and spray lightly, otherwise you may end up with paint drip marks. Not cute. Let the pot dry thoroughly between coats. It takes about fifteen minutes to dry completely. Three coats of paint should be sufficient.

MAKE AND BUILD

I will be the first to admit I don't always go about things in the most practical, ideal way. I'm more of a fly-by-the-seat-of-my-pants kind of girl. I've been known to hammer the wrong nails into sheet rock, use the wrong glue on wood, hold something together with a bent paperclip instead of wire—you get the gist. I'm more apt to spend twice the time jury-rigging something together with bits I have lying around rather than simply going to the store and buying proper materials. I have always been this way. I blame it on an incredibly resourceful father who used to drive by houses in our neighborhood real slowly the night before garbage day, cruising the piles of trash for hidden treasures. But there is an upside to my habits and heritage: making do with what I have and what I find has inspired some creative garden projects over the years.

Plenty of regular household items can be repurposed if you allow yourself to think big. Last year, I had the brilliant idea to hang a long, shallow planter box full of lettuce from clothes hangers. The concept was such that I could re-bend the wire frame of a hanger to hold the planter, then hang the planter from the hanger hook. It sounded smart, but in reality, it was a really terrible idea. The weight of all that soil immediately stretched the hook, and the planter came crashing down. Nonetheless, it is just this type of experiment that gets you thinking about how to use what you have. Hangers are a dime a dozen. Store-bought, hanging planter racks will set you back at least ten dollars. When you punch the numbers, it was a pretty economical project.

In the grand scheme of gardening, I do aim to be as thrifty as possible where I am able. Why purchase a bamboo teepee for my peas if I can just as easily fashion something out of sticks I find on walks around my neighborhood? (Not that I'm knocking bamboo stakes—they are a useful, great resource to have on hand.) I'm not terribly concerned with the garden looking perfect, and I find these small touches actually lend it quite a bit of character. I'm seldom organized enough to plan ahead. Frequently, it's this beauty of poor planning that leads to ingenuity. More often than not, I'm halfway through a project before I ever think about what I'm doing and then have to scramble to come up with a solution.

The do-it-yourself movement is firmly rooted in equal parts creativity, self-sufficiency, and sustainability. DIY projects are those that you make on your own, often with materials found, salvaged, or reused. These tasks rely as much on common sense and critical thought as on actual learned skills. My "toolbox" consists of one hammer and a small handsaw. If I need a screwdriver, I either call my neighbor or use a butter knife. Without the aid of an expert, DIY projects can revolutionize the way you think about your home. Sometimes this can make things slightly more difficult than they need to be, but I prefer that sort of hassle to others, (like trying to explain what I'm looking for at the hardware store by calling materials "thingys" and "whats-its"). I'm not one for a ton of research, and I don't want to have to reorganize my small closet spaces to accommodate more stuff. DIY is the perfect solution—the ultimate can-do! Using what you have on hand and getting creative, you can build, repair, and repurpose anything you desire. My main advice is to dig in and get it going.

These projects tend to be of the slap-it-together variety. I try to get away with the least amount of work possible. I don't want to spend half an afternoon crafting something. I just don't have a ton of extra time on my hands. Who does? So although I do make a conscious effort to slow down and smell the roses, I don't want to spend an entire day building the planter box to grow those roses in.

In truth, small apartment gardens don't require much in the way of materials. We have the privilege of living in the confines of a small space and therefore can make do with less. For urbanites, a successful garden is a matter of organization. If you fill your balcony with potted plants, you leave little space for much else. I like to have a few seats in my garden space—it's nice to have at least a small perch to sit on and observe nature. I also like to have certain tools and supplies handy at all times—a watering can, compost, seed-starting mix, and so on. Having access to these items is a nice reminder that I should do something: sow some seeds or transplant my fennel bulbs. If it is staring me in the face, I will take care of business. If I tuck something away, it's likely it will go unconsidered for a long while.

These projects have been inspired by need as well as thrift. To be perfectly honest, there may be a better or sounder way to approach some things, but I've come up with these quick ideas, and they have worked well for years. If it ain't broke, don't fix it! All in all, my hope is that this inventive approach leads to gardening inspiration. So often, people get stuck on what they need (but don't have) to get started or *how* they should get started. My suggestion, always, is to just get started. Don't worry about what you have or don't have—you'll make it work given what you have on hand and eventually figure out your own systems and fabricate your own projects.

Planter Box

This simple design is based on one large sheet of plywood, enough to make two smaller boxes. Plywood is not the strongest or best wood you can use for planter box materials, but it's cheap and functional. These boxes are built with the notion that you'll use them for only a couple of years before moving on to greener pastures, literally. I have designed these planter boxes to sit up on casters (wheels that attach to the underside) so you can roll them around as needed, and the space beneath the box allows for good drainage.

This is an easy afternoon project, but listen up: when you go to cut your lumber, you must cut it in a specific sequence, because something kooky will happen as you cut the wood. When you cut lumber, something called a *kerf* should be kept in mind. The kerf refers to the narrow proportion of wood you lose from the original piece from the width of the saw blade. In this instance the blade being used is generally ⅛-inch thick. To compensate for this loss, I have laid out a sequence of cuts to follow that take the kerf into account. In doing so, you will end up with a few small pieces of scrap lumber. Use them for signs or some other creative project.

The easiest way to get this job done and done right is to have your lumberyard cut the sections for you. Plywood is big and heavy and will need clamping and blocking in order to cut it properly. In short, it's a real hassle. Follow the diagram on page 144 and you'll be A-OK. Choose a lumberyard over a home improvement store. Most employees from these specialty shops will have the ability to adeptly handle the saw. Don't mess around with those who have not been formally trained.

You have options for the type of plywood you choose. The exterior grade I recommend is very rough and made to withstand the elements, but the surface will not be smooth. If you want a nice smooth finish because you intend to paint the exterior, choose a sanded plywood, which is slightly more expensive. The lumberyard staff should be able to walk you through your choices. Just be sure to purchase plywood that is ¾-inch thick.

Materials

- [ ] One sheet plywood—48 by 96 inches, ¾-inch thick, exterior grade (cut as illustrated on page 144; some wood will remain)

    Cut into:

    Four pieces of 35 by 15 inches

    Four pieces of 12 by 15 inches

    Two pieces of 36.5 by 12 inches

- [ ] Eight heavy-duty casters, each with 100 pounds capacity
- [ ] Thirty-two screws, ¾-inch long (be sure to match the size of the screw to the hole in the caster so it holds the caster in place properly)
- [ ] Eighty-four 1¾-inch coarse thread, exterior-grade decking screws
- [ ] Danish or orange oil

Directions

1. Separate your materials into two equal sets so that you have the same materials for each of your beds.

2. Enlist a friend to help you balance all of these pieces. On a flat and level work surface, stand a 35-by-15-inch piece of plywood on one long side. Stand up a 12-by-15-inch piece of plywood against the **outside edge** of the longer piece, matching up the 15-inch sides. Have your friend hold the two pieces snugly and squarely together. Next, drill four evenly spaced pilot holes to accommodate the screws. (A pilot hole is an initial smaller

MATERIALS

1 SHEET OF PLYWOOD

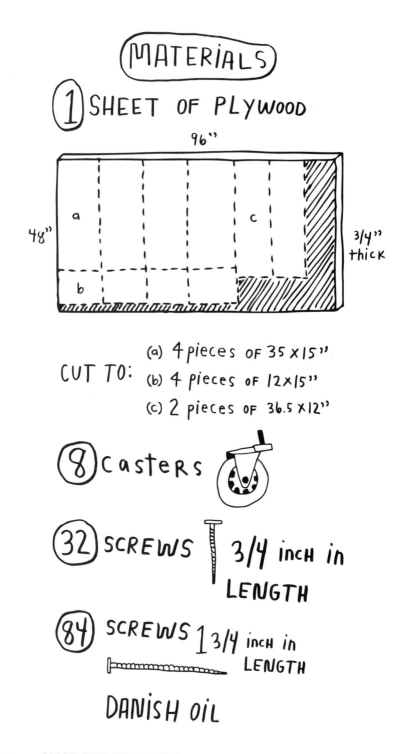

96"

48"

a

c

b

3/4" thick

CUT TO:
- (a) 4 pieces of 35 x 15"
- (b) 4 pieces of 12 x 15"
- (c) 2 pieces of 36.5 x 12"

8 casters

32 SCREWS 3/4 inch in LENGTH

84 SCREWS 1 3/4 inch in LENGTH

DANISH OIL

hole made in wood using a smaller drill bit, thereby preventing splitting when you drill in the screws.) Using a ³⁄₃₂-inch drill bit, drill through the 12-by-15-inch piece of wood into the larger piece. Try to drill as straight as possible, centering in the ¾-inch thickness, so you don't poke out of the side. After you've piloted the holes, screw the two pieces together using the 1¾-inch coarse thread decking screws. You now have the front and one side of the box attached.

3. Stand the other piece of 12-by-15-inch plywood against the opposite end of the longer piece, on its **outside edge**. Drill four pilot holes and screw together as on the other end. Fit the other 35-by-15-inch piece of plywood between the two side pieces and pilot and screw together in the same manner. Be sure to complete one side before moving to the last side. You now should have a bottomless wooden box made.

4. Next, decide which side will be the top and which the bottom. You want the bottom to be the side where all the corners best match up and lie nice and flat. Once you've chosen, flip the box upside down, so the bottom is facing up. Place a 36.5-by-12-inch piece over the box to form the bottom. You're going to evenly space nine screws along each long edge and four along each short edge. Working your way around the edge, pilot and then screw the button on.

5. Next, drill drainage holes into the bottom of the box using a ³⁄₈-inch drill bit. You will make two rows of holes every four inches across the bottom. There should be nine holes in each row. Space the rows four inches from the sides of the box. This should be adequate drainage.

6. Before you complete the box, add your casters to the corners of the bottom. Place each caster so its edge lines up with the edge of the box and screw in place (making smaller pilot holes first) with the shorter ¾-inch screws.

7. Your boxes will last longer if you apply a thin coat of oil before

planting. Oil helps give the wood a tough and slightly water-proof finish. Choose a Danish or orange oil from your local hardware store and apply two coats, letting them dry overnight, before filling with soil and planting.

8. To build the second box, repeat these steps!

Drying Rack

My friend Patric is a regular Mr. Fix-It. He taught me how to use an electric drill and build raised beds when I first starting my gardening business. He also happens to be a restaurateur, and his first restaurant was this beautiful Italian place that he practically built by hand. One afternoon, I was in the basement where they keep the prep tables for the kitchen. Behind the table where cooks were filling ravioli was an entire rack of screens used for drying the pasta. I took one look at them and immediately thought they would make awesome drying racks for leaves and seeds.

Drying out herbs and seeds is a fairly easy process, but it takes time and is more successful when you use drying racks. Air circulates around all sides of the plant, so they dry out faster and more evenly. Handmade drying racks can also be used for drying out tomatoes or fruits. And in the winter, you can use racks for laying out handmade pasta.

Although Patric made me my first set of racks, they are quite simple to make, and you can gather most materials from a quick trip to the hardware store. You can also keep your eyes open for salvaged wood. You will need to purchase a small length of screen, however. A densely woven chicken wire (¼-inch) or length of fine mesh screen will work well. Chicken wire works great for herbs (and pasta), whereas a screen (because it's woven so tightly) is best for drying out seeds. At your local hardware store, ask for chicken wire or window screen.

I like a large rack so I can spread out multiple stems simultaneously and not have them overlap. You can, of course, adjust the dimensions to fit your space.

For this project you are basically building two picture frames and sandwiching chicken wire between them. The two frames will have opposing joints, which will offer more support to the overall construction.

Materials

- ☐ Electric drill
- ☐ Staple gun
- ☐ Two 8-foot lengths of 1-by-2-inch furring strip—this is an untreated piece of timber available at any hardware store
- ☐ Eight 1¾-inch coarse-thread drywall screws
- ☐ Eight 2½-inch coarse-thread drywall screws
- ☐ Chicken wire or screen, cut to 23.5 by 17.5 inches. Use a good pair of scissors and be sure that you cut rough edges from the chicken wire. You do not want any jagged edges, so cut as close as you can to the outside wire, leaving a smooth edge.

Directions

1. Cut the following lengths from the furring strip using a handsaw or electric saw (you can also ask a salesperson at the hardware store to cut this for you):

    a. For the first frame, two 24-inch lengths of furring and two 16.5-inch lengths.

    b. For the second frame, two 22.5-inch lengths and two 18-inch lengths.

2. Assemble the frames: take both 24-inch furring strips and stand them up so they are on their narrow edge and sitting tall. Fit both the 16.5-inch pieces **in between** the 24-inch pieces, completing a frame-like shape. The overall dimension of your frame will be 24 by 18 inches.

3. Screw the frame together on all four corners, using the 1¾-inch screws. I recommend that you first drill a pilot hole, using a ³⁄₃₂-inch drill bit. You should now have one completed rectangular frame.

4. Repeat the same process using the 22.5-inch and 18-inch lengths. Make sure the 18-inch pieces are the outside pieces of your frame. (Slip the 22.5-inch pieces between the 18-inch pieces.) You will now have two frames of equal size.

5. Lay the chicken wire or screen across the back of one of the frames and anchor to the back of the frame with a staple gun in several places.

6. Sandwich the second frame on top of the chicken wire or screen so the sides are stacked and perfectly even.

7. Using the 2½-inch screws, screw the two frames together; be sure to make pilot holes first. Evenly space the screws, using two on each side of the frame.

If you're really not up for building anything, there are two other excellent options for a drying rack frame. One is shabby-chic and will look rad. The other is the laziest version imaginable, but it will work. The shabby-chic option makes use of old salvaged windows. Salvage yards have stacks of these, and they are typically pretty cheap. Choose a frame that is light and easy to lift and move around. I always opt for a brightly colored wooden frame with chipped paint. I love the look. Yes, old paint does tend to have lead in it, but you're not collecting or using the frame in any way conducive to ingesting paint chips. If you're genuinely concerned, it's best to build your own. Be sure to choose a frame made of a material that can be pierced with a staple gun—no ugly metal window frames!

Über-Chic Drying Screen

You can use a salvaged window frame or a picture frame for this project. With either, remove the glass pane. (You can use it as a cold frame for another garden project.) If using a picture frame, remove the cardboard backing as well. Stretch a length of screen taut across the back of the frame, leaving an inch of overhang. Starting in one corner, staple gun the screen to the back of the frame. Be sure to continue pulling the screen taut as you work. Trim any excess screen with a pair of sturdy scissors. To use as a drying rack, set the screen on top of four blocks, bricks, books, and so on. Raising it slightly allows for proper ventilation.

Über-Lazy Drying Screen

You can also use an old salvaged window screen. Salvaged goods depots often have these by the truckload. They are not the prettiest things, and you will need to set them up on blocks or bricks so air circulates underneath them, but they will work. If you go this route, be sure to wash your screen very, very well in hot soapy water followed by a dip in a bleach bath. Use one capful of bleach for every gallon of water. Screens used in construction are often quite dirty and may contain trace amounts of lead or other not-good-for-you elements. Know, also, that these thin screens can tear easily. Patric didn't think I should use them at all, due to their flimsiness, but they are completely functional. Just make sure not to bang them around too much. Use blocks or bricks to prop up the four corners. This allows for proper air circulation, which aids in more even drying and helps to prevent mold growing from moisture.

File Cabinet Planter

My friend Matthew Parker is one of those people who has vision. Everything in his funky little colorful house lines up and is orderly, but is also backed by wacky wall treatments like I found in his hallway—purple and white zigzag. He is utterly creative, and I steal hundreds of ideas from him.

We were chatting urban garden design ideas recently when he casually mentioned using an old file cabinet as a planter. A light bulb went off! Old metal file cabinets are easy to find at secondhand stores everywhere. They don't cost much—in the neighborhood of fifty bucks—and while they are ugly to look at, if you remove the drawers and turn them onto their backs, they make an awesome planter. File cabinets are deep, so you'll automatically have a deeper planter than you can buy retail without the hassle of making your own. Having a deep planter opens up your growing world quite a bit; you can start trying deep-rooted plants like tomatoes, kale, or rhubarb.

MATERIALS:

1.

2. WOOD

3. SPRAY PAINT

4. {PAINT!}

{JUST ADD PLANTS!}

5.

Casters

If you're into the whole shabby-chic thing, drawers can be used for shallow planters, as well. Just give them a coat of paint and plant away.

When repurposing any item, it is smart to consider possible pitfalls of what you are attempting. Or at least that's what my friend Patric is always telling me. He's awesome at identifying potential problems with all the crazy ideas I come up with. The looming obstacle for this project, so he says, is making sure the planter is structurally sound. Filing cabinets are made from thin sheet metal. You may have tried to stand on top of one at some point, to change a light bulb, only to feel the top buckle under your weight. Something similar will happen if you turn it on its back, and fill it with soil and then water. To address this, for this project we use a piece of *blocking wood*—a 2-by-4-inch piece of lumber cut to the width of the cabinet. The blocking wood both provides support and gives you a secure base to drill the casters into.

Materials

- One file cabinet
- Five or six locking and swiveling casters
- Four 1½-inch pan head screws appropriately sized for the holes in the casters
- Six to ten 1-inch pan head #8 screws
- One 2-by-4-inch by 8-foot board
- One small tube construction adhesive
- Four cans nontoxic primer spray paint
- Four cans nontoxic exterior gloss spray paint
- Electric drill with ⁷⁄₆₄-inch and ⅜-inch bits

Directions

1. Remove the drawers and any attached hardware from the inside of the cabinet. Measure its interior width. You will need to cut a few pieces of 2-by-4-inch boards to this length. The number of pieces depends on the size of the cabinet. A two-drawer cabinet will need three pieces: one on each end and one in the center. A three-drawer cabinet will need four

pieces: one on each end and two evenly spaced across the center. This wood support is called the blocking wood.

2. Cut the blocking wood so it fits snugly across the floor of the cabinet and rests squarely against the sides. Do not make it so tight that it causes the cabinet to bulge. (It is possible that the blocking wood pieces may have to vary slightly in size in order to get them to fit precisely.) Apply a few beads of construction adhesive to the blocking pieces and fit them into the cabinet. This is just to hold them in place—no need to go overboard with the glue. Allow them to dry for at least an hour.

3. Turn the cabinet over so the top is facing down and the bottom is facing up. Place casters in the corners of the cabinet, lining them up with the blocking wood. With a marker, trace the caster screw hole locations onto the cabinet and set the casters aside. Using the drill, make pilot holes where you've marked your casters through the cabinet and into the wood. Return the casters to the cabinet and screw them into place at the corners.

4. Now, add any supporting casters and place the casters along the middle of your cabinet. (For a two-drawer cabinet, you will also place a caster on the blocking in the center. For a three-drawer cabinet, you will need to place one caster on each piece of blocking.) Drill pilot holes, then screw the casters into place.

5. To keep the bottom of the cabinet from sagging under the weight of soil and water, you need to add some support. For support, you will add screws across the length of the center pieces of blocking wood. Adding screws in this manner effectively transfers the load (that is, the weight) across the cabinet floor to the edges, which are the cabinet's strongest points.

6. Using a ⁷⁄₆₄-inch drill bit, make pilot holes across the center pieces of blocking through the metal as you did for the casters. Start ½ inch from the edge of the cabinet. Drill pilot holes

every three inches until you run into the casters. It's not critical that the spacing be totally even. Finally, go back and add the screws for support.

7. Next, you need to make some drainage holes. Change the bit in your drill to ⅜-inch and drill through the cabinet, avoiding the blocking. You will need two rows of holes spaced every four inches or so.

8. In a well-ventilated area far removed from any objects you don't want subjected to drifting spray paint (such as your car or your neighbor's car), spray paint the exterior of the cabinet with two coats of primer and two coats of your finish color. You do not need to paint the entire interior of the cabinet, but make sure to get the first few inches around the edges, as soil will settle over time and expose the interior slightly. Also, be sure to let each coat dry completely before spray painting over. Finally, be sure to follow the instructions on the can, never holding the can too close. If you apply spray too thickly, it will run and create drip marks down your planter. (For specific instructions, see Spray-Painted Containers on page 139.)

9. When the planter is completely dry, it is ready for soil and plants! Make sure to lock your casters once you start filling your cabinet planter, and remember to fill the soil to the tip top of the planter. This allows for full sun to hit the surface of your soil—a crucial step in germination.

(Patric's construction note: When someone is talking to you about building something and trying to intimidate you with big words like *blocking*, *bracing*, or *transferring loads*, you will now know what they are talking about.)

Hanging Planter

I love the idea of wirework because it is such an easy afternoon project using material ripe for repurposing. Bend some hangers, fashion them together in some way, and voilà!—mission accomplished. I played with hangers for quite some time before I perfected the concept of a hanging planter. You need to work with a smallish pot so the weight of the soil doesn't pull the hanger down. This hanging system is meant to get plants up and off your patio to make room for more pots that are too heavy to hang. With this technique, you can hang small pots off your railings to maximize space.

Materials

- [ ] Two wire hangers
- [ ] Needle-nose pliers
- [ ] 1 small terra-cotta pot

Directions

1. Using the pliers, clip the hooks off the tops of the hangers. Straighten all bends in the remaining wire to form a straight line. Wrap one of these tightly around the pot's circumference, just under the collar. This creates a wire loop around your pot. Twist the ends to create a close-fitting wire loop around the pot. You will have about a 9-inch length of hanger slack left.

2. Using the second hanger, with the length of the wire vertical, loop one end under the first wire hoop, directly opposite the 9-inch remainder. Make a bend in the wire, about 3 inches down, then twist it around the longer piece of hanger to secure. At this point, you should have about 25 inches of wire remaining on the second hanger.

3. Join the remaining wire lengths from both sides in the middle and twist to secure them together. Using the remaining 16 inches or so of the second hanger, wrap around your banister

or railing and secure by looping tightly. Voilà! A quick hanging plant system.

Tools of the Trade

When you have a small apartment garden focused on growing food in containers, a big ol' garden rake is not going to be useful to you. In a small-scale garden environment, you need small-scale tools. Rather than investing money in a trowel or spade, you can perform the same tasks with simple kitchen items: one fork, one spoon, and one measuring cup.

Fork

Forks are great for digging in fertilizer and compost. Sprinkle some fertilizer or compost on the top of the soil, around the base of the plant. Use your fork to dig it into the first few inches of potting soil. Forks may also be used to lightly mix in seeds when sowing directly into a pot. Flower and looseleaf lettuce seeds can be sprinkled directly onto the potting soil surface. Using your fork, lightly pick over them and turn the soil gently. This light forking works well for small seeds that need only to be surface sown.

Spoon

A spoon is an obvious substitute for a shovel or trowel. When you are working with pots of soil, you don't need to do much digging. At most, you will need to dig down a few inches in the outer edges of the pot to check for moisture levels. To do this, rather than using a spade (which will actually displace too much soil), choose a soup spoon. The narrow handle is perfect for digging down deeply without disturbing the roots of the plant. In containers, root systems tend to press up against container walls and weave themselves in spirals at the bottom of the pot. You don't want to do too much damage to them, and a rounded spoon is soft enough that it won't invade the roots' space. Spoons are also great for removing moss-covered soil from pots. After winter, when some of the pots may be covered with dewy green moss, use the spoon as a skimmer to remove the moss from the pot. Replace the soil with fresh compost. I also use spoons to scoop out cigarette butts that visitors to my little garden can't seem to resist putting out in my plants! I spoon out about an inch of soil around each cig. Necessary? Probably not. But it makes me feel better, and I like to freshen up the soil now and again anyway.

Measuring Cup

A measuring cup does the job that a shovel or trowel would do in a "real" garden. Because you are adding only small amounts of potting soil to plants, the measuring cup allows for precision and also prevents too much soil from being dusted all over your patio as you work. Use a large measuring cup to scoop up and fill in potting soil for plants. When potting a new plant start, pour a few inches of potting soil into the pot, then add your start. Use the measuring cup to lightly sprinkle soil around the sides of the plant start, until your pot is filled.

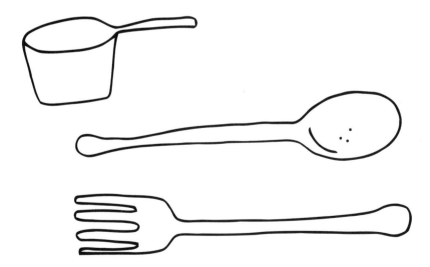

Water Bottle Redux

Never one to toss something out without first considering how I can use it, I have made plastic water bottles the tool du jour in my garden. I use them to water my plants, protect seedlings, and, in a pinch, act as a drip system when I'm away for some time.

A *cloche* is a protective dome of plastic or glass that insulates plants and protects them from inclement weather so that they are able to grow with vigor. The original cloches were bell jars, beautiful glass domes with ventilation at the top. Cloches are set directly over individual plants, where they trap in heat from the sun and protect from wind, rain, and even some pests. You can emulate the concept of a bell jar by using a water jug or bottle.

A drip system or sprinkler is a timed watering mechanism for gardens. Obviously, most apartment gardens will not have a drip system, and there is not always a willing neighbor to water when you're away. In the heat of summer, it is crucial that your plants receive regular water. You do not want the soil to dry out—it will grow hard and will not allow water to pass through evenly. To prevent this, set up a slow drip water system when you're gone and no one is around to pitch in. It's not a perfect solution, but it's a good one.

Here are the how-to's for reusing and recycling water bottles in the garden.

Water Bottle Cloche

Trim off the bottom of your water jug or bottle as close to the bottom as possible. Set the water bottle directly over seedlings or starts and push the cut rim into the soil to anchor. Leave the cap off to allow for ventilation.

Water Bottle Watering

Use a water bottle with a cap. Trim the bottom off the bottle. Take the water bottle cap and pierce a hole in the top with a small nail and a hammer. You can also use a thin drill bit (about ⅛ inch). Test for drainage by putting water in the open end of the water bottle and holding it upside down. The water should come out at a slow trickle—a drop every few seconds. Submerge the water bottle, cap side down, into your pot. Fill the bottom with water to the rim. Refill as needed.

Worm Bin

As explained in Chapter 5, Feeding & Watering Plants, worms are awesome garden helpers that not only fertilize your plants but also take care of kitchen waste for you. When you live in a small space, there is often no place to start a compost pile. Worms in a worm bin take care of this, breaking down organic matter that you add to their bin and producing what we call worm castings. These castings can then be used to dress and fertilize your pots.

Worms will multiply over time; when this happens, you can remove extras and pass them along to friends and neighbors. You can also try to sell them to other local gardeners: this could turn into your own mini-business, based off waste from solely your kitchen.

I've seen several versions of worm bins over the years. I prefer the tall, stacked wood variety, but for a patio it is best to use a plastic bin. It prevents drippings and excess moisture from getting onto your patio and is small enough to fit without overwhelming your space. You can also move your worm bin indoors—and you may have to do this in winter if the temperatures drop to freezing. Worm bins should not give off an unpleasant odor (if yours does, you have a problem) so they are OK to have indoors.

When selecting a container, make sure to choose a dark plastic, so that light cannot penetrate the sides. Your worm bin will need proper ventilation for the worms. Drill holes into the sides and lid of the worm bin for air and in the bottom for drainage. The bin sits in an inverted plastic lid, which will collect any excess liquid that drains

MATERIALS:

1. PLASTIC STORAGE BOX, ABOUT 1 FOOT DEEP & 2 FEET LONG, PLUS 2 LIDS

2. NEWSPAPER, Black & White PRINT ONLY, SHREDDED

3. 1 POUND OF RED WIGGLER WORMS

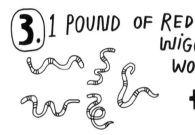

+ HANDFUL OF TOPSOIL OR SAND

4. DRILL TEN AIR HOLES AROUND THE TOPSIDES OF YOUR BIN

5. + H₂O SOAK YOUR NEWSPAPER, FILL YOUR BIN & ADD WORMS.

6. DON'T FORGET TO ADD KITCHEN WASTE!

7. HARVEST! & ENJOY!

from the bin. This liquid is considered a compost "tea" and can be added directly to your potted plants.

Materials

- [ ] Plastic storage box, about 1 foot deep and 2 feet long, plus 2 lids
- [ ] Newspaper, black and white print only, shredded
- [ ] 1 pound of red wiggler worms
- [ ] Handful of topsoil or sand

Directions

1. Using an electric drill fitted with a ½-inch bit, drill ten air holes around the top sides of the bin and five air holes in the cover. Finally, drill ten drainage holes in the bottom of the bin. Leave the second lid intact to serve as a drainage tray.

2. Prepare the worm bedding by soaking shredded newspaper in water and wringing it out. You want your newspaper to be moist, but not soaking—the classic comparison is "as damp as a wrung-out sponge." Fill the bin until the newspaper is about eight inches deep. The bedding should be moist and fluffy, not heavy and compact. Add a handful of topsoil or sand. This helps the worms to digest their food. Set the bin on top of the inverted second lid.

3. Now add the worms to the middle of the bedding. Lift a few layers and drop them in. You should also add a handful of kitchen waste and cover it well with bedding. By keeping the top layer of bedding clean at all times, you minimize odors and the risk of attracting fruit flies and other pests.

4. Keep your worm bin in a cool, shady place outside or underneath your kitchen sink. You want to keep the worms at their favored temperature range of 55 to 75 degrees.

5. Worms eat nearly their own weight in kitchen waste every day. For 1 pound of worms, count on adding about 5 pounds of kitchen waste each week. You may add any vegetative food

scraps, spent coffee grounds, and crushed eggshells to the worm bin. Do not add protein scraps (meat or fish) or any oils.

6. Worms will eat kitchen scraps and most of the original bedding in about four months' time. Replenish the bedding as needed to keep added food scraps covered. As described in Chapter 5, Feeding & Watering Plants, to harvest the worm compost, move the entire contents of the bin to one side of your bin. Add fresh, moist bedding and kitchen scraps to the other side of the bin. The worms will slowly migrate over to the new bedding and food. This can take anywhere from about three to six weeks. When all the worms have migrated over, you can harvest the compost and add it to your pots as fertilizer, shifting the new bedding into place across the bin when you are finished.

7. Worm compost is high in nitrogen, so be careful to only add small amounts to your pots. A couple of spoonfuls in each pot is sufficient.

Chapter 8

Garden Lite

L et's face it, gardening isn't for everyone. Even if you're interested in growing food at home, if you have a crazy schedule and you really don't want to be responsible for tending to something on a daily basis, gardening may not be for you. Or it could be that your space is not conducive to gardening. Some yards and patios get so little sun that the renter's only hope for farm-fresh produce is a weekly visit to the farmers' market. That is OK. No sense in trying to jam a square peg into a round hole. There are lots of other options for you that are super simple. They may not fill up dinner plate after dinner plate, but they can add small fresh touches to your meals and help you feel like you're growing *something* green.

Microgreens

Microgreens are all the rage with chefs, and you've likely eaten them without even knowing it. Teeny tiny plants that are only two to three weeks old and have only two true sets of leaves are considered microgreens. These little plants are easily identified by taste—they pack a flavor punch. Many vegetables make tasty microgreens that can be used as garnish on dishes. You don't want to cook these; the flavor is too delicate to withstand heat. But they're great as a finishing flavor to your meals—sprinkled over seared fish or grilled meat. What's more, microgreens are ready to eat in just a few weeks. This short time frame fits the needs of many busy urbanites. Microgreens need very little attention and can be grown right in a baking dish on your windowsill. As you are not going to be concerned about the overall health of the plants, even with limited natural light you need not worry about feeding them. You barely even need to water microgreens. Just keep a spray bottle handy and keep the seeds moist until they germinate.

How to Start a Microgreen Garden

Use a shallow baking dish or roasting pan and fill it almost to the top with seed-starting mix. Broadcast the seeds densely across the surface of the mix. Spray with a water bottle to saturate the surface. Cover with plastic wrap to hold in moisture and create some heat. Place in a windowsill. Keep the mix moist and lift the wrap to ventilate the dish every few days. In just a few days you will see your greens sprouting. Wait until they reach one to two inches tall and have two true leaves to harvest. Cut as close to the soil as possible. When you've harvested the whole tray, start again. You should be able to use the same seed-starting medium two or three times before having to refresh. If it ever grows moldy from excess moisture, toss it out and replenish with fresh seed-starting mix.

SEEDS FOR MICROGREENS		
Arugula	Celery	Parsley
Basil	Cilantro	Radish
Beets	Cucumber	Sorrel

Sprouts

You likely think of sprouts as those dense and wiry, tasteless greens that people insist on using on vegetable sandwiches. There was a time when you couldn't eat at a deli without seeing the ubiquitous vegetarian sandwich offering: cream cheese, cucumber, and alfalfa sprouts. (Personally, these never did much for me, though I know many folks love them.) Sprouts, however, can be delicious, and I've lately seen them crop up more and more in restaurants and groceries.

Sprouts are essentially the very first growth a seed puts out before it develops true leaves. Mung bean sprouts are a great example of what a sprout looks and tastes like. Sprouts add a fresh crispy texture to dishes and are packed with nutrients. Seeds store all the energy and food they need to produce healthy plants. By eating them at a very early stage of growth, we reap the rewards of all that good energy.

Different sprouts will carry different flavors, of course. Legumes like peas or mung beans produce thick, crunchy sprouts. Broccoli and alfalfa sprouts are more delicate and won't have as much flavor. Alliums like onions and scallions are a bit slimy feeling, but they taste very strongly of onion. Play around a bit and see what you like.

Sprouts are, by far, some of the easiest things to "grow" at home. No soil and no windowsill required, and the entire process takes anywhere from three to five days. You need only a quart-size glass jar to get going. Basically, you give seeds a moist environment and rinse them every few hours. Some sources say to cover the jar on your counter to avoid photosynthesis so the sprout doesn't develop a leaf, while some say it doesn't matter.

I've done it both ways with success, but I tend to cover the jar. If I want small greens, I plant seeds as a microgreen instead.

HOMEGROWN SPROUTS	
Alfalfa	Mung Bean
Broccoli	Onion
Chickpea	Pea
Leek	Red Clover
Lentil	Sunflower

Materials

- [ ] One large jar
- [ ] 1 teaspoon bleach
- [ ] Water
- [ ] ¼ cup seeds
- [ ] Small length of cheesecloth

Directions

1. Disinfect seeds (a necessary step, as some may carry *E. coli*). Combine one teaspoon of bleach with 1 cup of tap water and let ¼ cup of seeds soak for 15 minutes. Drain and rinse thoroughly three times.

2. Place the clean seed in the bottom of the jar.

3. Fill the jar with 1 cup of water.

4. Cover the jar with a double layer of cheesecloth and secure with a rubber band. This allows for air circulation.

5. Let the seeds soak overnight in a dark cupboard (away from light).

6. In the morning, pour off all the water, making sure none of it pools inside. You can leave the jar (with the cheesecloth still intact) upside down on a plate or bowl to ensure drainage.

7. Hold the drained jar horizontally and shake gently to distribute the seeds along the side of the jar. Place on its side and cover with a dishtowel to block out light for about 4 hours.

8. Rinse the jar with fresh water two or three times a day, every day. Drain each time and set back on its side.

9. The sprouts should be ready to harvest in 3 to 5 days. Taste them after every rinse to see when the flavor has developed to your taste.

10. Fill the jar with water for the last time and remove any thick hulls (the outer covering of the seeds).

11. Drain the sprouts in a colander and eat immediately, or wrap in single layer of dishtowel or paper towel and hold in the refrigerator, where they will keep for 4 to 7 days.

The Wild Garden: Foraged Food for the Urbanite

A few years ago, I was driving to a dinner party with friends. It was a potluck, and we were all balancing dishes on our laps and between our feet in the car. I had just picked up my friend Mark Brack, and as I drove down the road, I was thinking about dinner. Up ahead I saw some wild fennel growing on the left side of the road. Without missing a beat, I rolled down my window, slowed down the car, and without a pause in the conversation, reached out my hand and grabbed a clump of fennel fronds. What seemed like a perfectly normal thing to do at the time (hey—I needed garnish!) shocked everyone into silence, immediately followed by a burst of laughter. Not exactly the most traditional way to forage for food, but it worked!

Many urban areas are fecund with wild edible food, and you need not take a day hike into the mountains to find it. I embellish my pantry with food collected when I'm out and about doing errands or taking a walk. My eyes are now trained to scan any vegetation I walk by for its edible potential. First and foremost, it's thrifty! Food doesn't get much more affordable than when you're collecting from the wild. And second, the flavors found in nature are markedly different from those of most cultivated crops. They tend to be stronger, bolder, and more pronounced. I like the challenge of cooking with flavors I'm unaccustomed to. I am also attracted to the idea that I can walk out my front door and gather some food for lunch.

Many are intimidated by the idea of foraging until they've tried it. But there is plenty of guidance out there for beginners. There are field guides and books dedicated to the craft. Although I love the idea of foraging for my food, the truth is I'm a city girl, and if I don't find something on the walk from my car to a restaurant (or while driving down the street), the odds of my collecting wild edibles are slim. I also don't trust myself enough to safely identify all sorts of plants in the wild. Sometimes I can't tell the difference between chickweed and peppercress, and although you can eat both of them, properly identifying greens can be stressful because certain details are very important but not always easy to distinguish. However, there are lots of plants that grow along sidewalks, in neighborhood greenbelts, and in parks where urbanites often go for some R&R that are easily identifiable. These plants are a great introduction to the practice of foraging, and you need only keep an eye out as you make your way about the city.

As with any collected wild foods, you should never harvest anything you are uncertain of. Additionally, as city property can often be sprayed with pesticides, you want to make certain to wash anything you collect before eating. But it's a small price to pay for an economical and flavorful harvest.

Foraging is also a great afternoon adventure for lazy gardeners who just can't get it together. You know who you are! Not everyone has time to think about what to grow and when. But we all have to eat! Foraging is a nice happy medium—you are still harvesting, still collecting homegrown food, just not food that you grew yourself at your home. A friend asked me once, "What is the laziest gardening tip ever?" And the laziest tip I could think of is to forage from the urban gardens that surrounds us every day. You don't have to do a bloody thing to forage for food. No watering, no feeding of plants. It's just you, a collecting bag, and maybe a stick to hack through any serious berry brambles.

Following is a list of easy-to-identify and easy-to-gather urban edibles, in order of season.

Stinging Nettles

Nettles are hot hot hot these days. Known for their superfood properties (nettles are rich in vitamins A, C, and D and loaded with calcium and even protein), everyone wants to get their hands on some. But be careful—raw nettles will sting you if they come in contact with your skin. The leaves and stem have tiny plant hairs that penetrate your skin and result in welts that sting and burn slightly and are sometimes itchy. Luckily, the welts don't last for long on most people. Nettles grow along roadsides and pathways, mostly in woods, so keep your eyes open when you're on any urban nature walks. They come up first thing at the end of winter and are best harvested around March when they are still young, one to two feet high. The leaves are deeply serrated and end with a pointed tip. They grow in tiers like a Christmas tree—big leaves at the bottom of the plant and smaller leaves toward the tip. Nettles tend to grow in clusters. If you're not sure you've found nettles, a light brush up against a leaf will quickly confirm any suspicions. Nettles are mildly flavored and can be used as a hearty green, a filling for pastas or roulades, or a quick pesto-like pasta sauce. Nutrient-dense nettle leaves may also be used in the garden as an all-purpose fertilizer for your plants—they are thought to pass their beneficial qualities on to other plants.

To harvest, wear gloves and trim only the top foot of the stem and leaves. Clip with scissors and place in a large paper bag. When home, set a large pot over high heat and just cover the bottom with water, about ¼ cup. When the water is boiling, toss in the nettles and steam for 10 to 12 minutes. This will remove the sting and leave them ready for eating. Nettles can be used as you would spinach or sauted greens in recipes. You can also leave the nettles on their stalks and lay them out on drying racks or hang them upside down to dry. These dried leaves can be steeped as tea, which is thought to be rich in minerals and vitamins.

To make nettle tea for your garden, fill a large jar or jug densely with nettle leaves and cover in water. Let sit out, covered, for a little over a week. During this time, the leaves will start to ferment. The mixture will smell a bit boozy and yeasty. Spray on plants or add a cupful to each container once a week.

Dandelion

Poor dandelion, always getting a bad rap for wreaking havoc on lawns and in general being a ruthless weed. It's true that dandelions are a deeply rooted "weed" that are nearly impossible to dig out, but it's also true that they taste pretty good and are literally everywhere. One need not look very far to find a bed of dandelions fit for eating; they are easily identifiable. Dandelion greens turn bitter and woody quite quickly, so very early spring is the best time to harvest them. Try to clip the small leaves from the plant before the plant flowers. Once the yellow flower has bloomed, taste the greens first to see if you find the flavor too off-putting. Harvest by picking off the small leaves and eating straight away. Be sure to wash dandelion greens well, and steer clear of picking them out of public lawns. Those areas are too heavily sprayed with chemicals to warrant eating. Use dandelion greens in salads, or cook them in a sauté. I like my greens wilted with a little bacon and an egg in the morning. You may also use the flower petals in recipes. I roll chopped petals into cracker or pie dough, for their bright yellow color, but the taste will not shine through unless you use an exorbitant amount of petals.

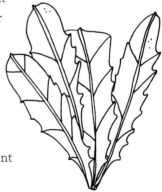

Watercress

Watercress is easily identifiable by a novice for two reasons. First, it grows directly on small riverbeds and streams, practically on top of the water. Second, wild watercress looks very much like the watercress you find at the grocery. Pay attention the next time you're in the store, and you'll be sure to identify the plant in the wild. While our cityscapes don't typically have lazy streams running through them, there are plenty of water tributaries in parks and ditches along the sides of roads that collect water. Look there and you'll likely find some watercress. Watercress has a hollow succulent stem and an arugula-like leaf. It grows right at the water's edge. Cut the stem just below the water's surface for the fullest harvest. At home, be sure to wash the watercress several times, as running water can carry bacteria or parasites. If eating raw, you may want to take extra precautions and rinse your watercress in a bleach solution—one tablespoon per gallon. If you go this route, rinse with fresh water three times in succession after the bleach rinse; then the watercress is safe to eat.

Fennel Blossoms

Wild fennel looks very much like the fennel fronds you see in the grocery and at farmers' markets, though wild fennel is not a bulbing variety. Instead, wild fennel grows tall and vigorous in the wild, offering up licorice-scented fronds nearly year-round that can be harvested and used as a fresh herb. In summer, the stalks from the fennel plant will flower bright yellow, tight petal clusters. These blossoms have a distinct fennel flavor without the sharpness that is found in both green and mature seeds. In early fall, seeds from the plant may also be harvested. Immature green fennel seeds come in immediately following the blossoms around late August and early September. These seeds can be eaten raw and have a crisp fennel bite. Mature seeds are available in early fall and, much like the fennel seeds you purchase in the store, they can be used to stock your spice larder.

To collect fennel blossoms, wait until the blossoms are in full bloom and open. Flower heads will be densely packed and bright yellow. Cut stems just below flower bunches—each stem will have a multitude of blossoms. Do not rinse them off! While fennel blossoms are often collected from roadsides and railroad tracks, rinsing them will remove some of the pollen that you're trying to collect. To dry the blossoms, make a small bouquet and secure with a long piece of string or twine. Put the blossom end of the bouquet in a paper bag, so the stems are facing up and sticking out of the bag's opening. Bunch up the paper bag opening around the stems and tie closed with the extra twine. Hang upside down in a dry location. Drying fennel blossoms like this ensures that all the flowers and pollen will be collected, as it will sometimes drop during drying. After three to four weeks, the blossoms should be completely dry. Remove the bag and pick off the blossoms with your fingertips. To do this, set up a clean workstation and, holding the stem in one hand, pull up on each individual blossom stem to release the flowers. You may also cut with a pair of scissors, being careful not to also cut the small stem. Store blossoms in a small glass jar in your spice cupboard, where they will keep for several months or longer.

Blackberries

Juicy berries ripen from June through September in most climates, and many are native or grow in the wild. Blackberries, in particular, grow rampant in many parts of the country. Big juicy fruit berries follow white flowers that grow on thick, thorned vines that tend to climb up and over all other vegetation, searching for sun. There are native North American blackberries, but most of those we find in urban landscapes are the Himalayan species, which is considered an invasive plant. This means that many people hate blackberries and try to remove the bramble thickets from their landscape. Blackberries grow on the sides of roads and along walkways in many of our parks. The best berries, as always, will be the ones off the beaten track that aren't available with a simple stretch of the arm. Additionally, with berries that grow back a bit from any public spaces, there is less of a chance that they've been sprayed. When collecting blackberries, use a medium-sized bowl so the fruits don't get squished and beaten to pulp in a plastic bag. At home, fill the entire bowl with cold water and give them a gentle toss with your hands. Rinse and repeat three times, finally laying them on a dish towel (or a paper towel if you don't want to stain your dish towel) to dry.

Rose Hips

Rose hips are the seed buds that follow the rose blooms. *Rosa rugosa* plants make hips somewhere between late July and September. You can identify these bushes when in bloom by their strong rose-scented flowers, which bloom in white, pinks, and bright fuchsia. Make note of their location and head back in about four weeks to collect the rose hips, or wait until just after the first frost which is thought to make the rose hips sweeter. Rose hips look like little tomatoes, often orange-red and shiny. They are more round than long, about the size of a red globe grape. Harvest rose hips by snapping the stem from the plant. They are tough enough that you can toss them into a plastic bag and then a backpack without doing too much damage. Rinse them well when you get home to drown out any bugs and use them within a day of bringing them home. Rose hip purée can be made and frozen and used later in recipes.

Apples and Plums

There are fruit trees tucked all over most urban landscapes. You need only look up and pay attention in the height of the summer, when most trees are setting fruit. Or look down on the ground to see what fruit is falling come late summer and early fall. Apple and plum trees are the most prominent, though I've seen pears, quince, and cherries among many city landscapes where I've lived. Just keep your eyes open! Tree fruit is easily turned into jams, butters, and pastes. Boil down with sugar (to taste) and store in a glass jar in your refrigerator. Plums are delicious in upside-down cakes, as they release enough juice to make a sticky, sugary delight on the bottom of the pan (and top of the cake). Soft fruits, like plums, are also lovely to preserve in spirits.

Walnuts

Walnut trees are found growing tall and broad in many cities. Rather than look for the tree, I always keep my eyes on the ground and look for old nuts or husks from last year's crop. Walnuts drop their nuts around September; at this point they are wrapped in a bright green, soft husk, looking almost like a smooth, light green lime. In time these husks rot and fall away, exposing the hard shell of a walnut. When handling walnuts in their husks, be sure to wear gloves, as they will stain your bare hands. I learned this the hard way and walked around with blackened palms for weeks one summer. Walnuts must be cured before cracking or you'll have a hard time removing the nut meat from the shell. Leave them in a box in a warm, dry place for several weeks, or dry them out at a very low temperature in the oven overnight.

Resources

There is a breadth of information available for anyone interested in food, growing food, and cooking at home, but these are some of my favorite resources that I reference time and time again. These sources get to the heart of the matter and provide enough information for you to make your own decisions about gardening, small urban farm projects, preserving, and cooking.

Growing Food at Home

GoGo Green Garden
www.gogogreengarden.com
My blog about all things homegrown.

Urban Garden Share
www.urbangardenshare.org
Share your yard or find some space to grow with this network of experienced and aspiring gardeners and home-owners.

Renewing America's Food Traditions
www.slowfoodusa.org/index.php/programs/details/raft
Save our seeds! Seeds are a precious resource—learn how to save them.

Organic Seed Alliance

www.seedalliance.org

A great resource for locating organic seed for veggies and flowers.

Rodale's Ultimate Encyclopedia of Organic Gardening

By the editor of *Organic Gardening and Farming Magazine* (New York: Rodale, 2009)

I have the vintage version (*The Encyclopedia of Organic Gardening*, 1976), passed down from my father. It is a must for scientific plant information.

Scented Geraniums

www.killdeerfarms.com

Killdeer Farms is one of the few resources with a bounty of scented geraniums, and you can order online and have plants shipped.

Urban Homesteading

Quillisascut Farm School

www.quillisascut.com

Worth the trip to Washington's farm country, "Quilla" changed my life and offers week-long farm immersions to introduce and connect people to their food.

American Beekeeping Federation

www.abfnet.org

A great place to start gathering info on beekeeping at home.

Puget Sound Beekeepers Association

www.pugetsoundbees.org

Check out the Puget Sound Beekeepers Association for a local Pacific Northwest resource on beekeeping.

The River Cottage Cookbook

By Hugh Fearnley-Whittingstall (Berkeley: Ten Speed Press, 2008)

www.rivercottage.net

Homesteading perfection in a thick book with beautiful photos by Simon Wheeler.

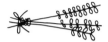

Cooking and Food

Foodista

www.foodista.com

An online cooking encyclopedia anyone can edit with pictures, articles, and recipes, this is a great resource for home cooks wanting to engage in a cooking community.

Farmers Markets and Local Food Marketing

www.ams.usda.gov/AMSv1.0/farmersmarkets

Support your local food producers and small family farms!

Preserving

National Center for Home Food Preservation

www.uga.edu/nchfp

All the rules you could ever hope to know about safe home canning—plus some decent recipes!

Cooperative Extension Programs

www.csrees.usda.gov/Extension

Find your local program, and you'll find a TON of useful information about home food preservation and local agriculture.

Index

S

sage, 34, 129
salts, herbal, 132–33
salvaged materials, 14–16, 137–38, 148–49
salves, 131
scented geraniums, 4–5, 48, 61, 97, 106–7, 109, 127, 134, 176
seed saving, 54–55, 175
seed starting, 56–61
  choosing seeds, 53–56, 176
  general discussion, 56–59
  hardening off seedlings, 4, 61
  making plant labels, 136
  microgreens, 12, 164
  protective covers, 19, 59, 60–61, 157
  in sacks or bags, 16
  seed-starting mix, 57, 59, 60
  step-by-step guide, 59–61
  tools for, 155
  See also propagation; specific plant
seed trays, 59, 60, 61
seeds, edible, 5, 83–84, 112–14, 119–20, 132, 133
self-seeding annuals, 5, 62
shade, providing, 19, 20
shade-tolerant herbs, 38
silverware, as plant labels, 137–38
slugs, 19, 68
small plants for small pots, 12
snap peas, 30
soil, 16–18
  amendments, 4
  choosing, 16–17

general discussion, 1–2
perennials, 17–18
seed-starting mix, 57, 59, 60
tools for, 155–56
top-dressing, 5, 17, 67, 76
See also feeding and fertilizing; mulches
spirits, herb-infused, 135
spoons, 155–56
spray-painted containers, 139, 153
sprouts, 165–67
squashes. *See* zucchini
starts versus seed starting, 57–58
stinging nettles, 169–70
stones, as plant labels, 137
strawberries, 12, 30–31, 106–7
sugar petals, making, 109
sunlight requirements, 7, 38, 58, 59, 60

T

taproots, 23
tarragon, 61, 81–82, 96
"teas," compost, 76, 158, 160
teas, herbal, 134
terra-cotta pots, 9
thyme, 41–42, 61, 97, 100–1, 129, 130–31, 133
tisanes, 134
toner, facial, 126–27
tools for small-scale gardening, 155–56
top-dressing, 5, 17, 67, 76
transplanting, 18, 61, 63
trellises, 19

V

vegetables. *See* fruits and vegetables

vegetative propagation, 62
vermiculture and vermicompost, 74

W

walnuts, foraging for, 173–74
water bottle redux, 157–58
watercress, foraging for, 171
watering, 12
  checking moisture with a spoon, 155
  container material, 9, 10, 13, 14, 16
  schedule for, 8, 76–78
  seed starting, 59, 60–61
  self-watering system, 157–58
  soil retention, 17, 72, 73, 76
  under-/over-watering, 25, 76–78
wild edibles, foraging for, 5–6, 167–74
winter. *See* mulches; overwintering
wooden boxes, as planters, 13–14, 15–16, 142–46
worm bins, 74–76, 158–61

Z

zucchini, 32, 78, 81–82, 97, 101–3

About the Author

Food enthusiast **Amy Pennington** is the creator and owner of GoGo Green Garden, an edible garden business wherein she builds, plants, and tends edible gardens for city folk in their backyards. In March 2009, Amy launched UrbanGardenShare.org, a garden website that pairs city gardeners with unused garden space via an online matching site.

Amy has been featured on Martha Stewart Living Radio's *Whole Living* program, and in national and international publications, including *Woman's Day* magazine and the *Toronto Star*. She is a regular contributing writer to *Edible Seattle*, a bi-monthly, food-focused magazine highlighting the culinary bounty of the Puget Sound region. Her first book, *Urban Pantry*, was published in early 2010 and was chosen as one of the top ten cookbooks in Amazon.com's Best Books of 2010. She lives in Seattle. Visit www.gogogreengarden.com to learn more.